Praise for *The Trading Mindwheel*

"Excellent! *The Trading Mindwheel* is packed with many practical steps needed to become a more successful trader. It's perfect for anyone who's read Reminiscences of a Stock Operator (Lefevre/Livermore) and William O'Neil's book (*How to Make Money in Stocks*) and is ready for more specifics. If you are serious about speeding up your learning curve, this is a great addition to your trading library."

—Mike Webster,
Prior: IBD-Head Market Strategist,
O"Neil Capital Mgmt-SVP/PM Ideas.
Current Portfolio Manager for a private fund

"Mike explains trading psychology in a way that every trader can not only grasp but instantly apply to their trading. The tips and techniques that Mike shares are not going to be found in some random online blog; Mike has such a unique way of explaining things that you're sure to find value in every sentence. Mike has been around long enough to know what works and what doesn't work, and he conveys that incredibly well."

—Austin Silver,
Founder ASFX.biz

"In his book, *The Trading Mindwheel*, Michael emphasizes the vital role mindset plays in a trader's ability to profitably execute a sound trading strategy. Top-performing traders know that achieving trading mastery first requires overcoming mental barriers."

—Leif Soreide,
2019 US Investing Champion and
Founder of Champion Team Trading

"Michael Lamothe is the real deal. He is living proof that dreams do come true on Wall Street. He quit his nine-to-five and now makes a full-time living from the stock market. Michael knows what it takes to be successful on and off Wall Street. Michael does a great job of simplifying complicated topics that most people do not talk about when it comes to investing and trading stocks. The proper mindset required to be successful on Wall Street is arguably the most important element that separates the smart money from everyone else. Traders at nearly all levels can benefit from Michael's work. I recommend Michael to just about anyone looking to get ahead! Keep up the great work!"

—Adam Sarhan,
Author of *Psychological Analysis*, Host of
The Smart Money Show Podcast, *Forbes* Contributor,
and Founder FindLeadingStocks.com

"*The Trading Mindwheel* covers important concepts that all traders should know and implement in their trading. It's an excellent resource for new and experienced traders alike!"

—Rizwan Memon,
Founder and President Riz International

"As a longtime buy-and-hold investor, I found this book to be a fascinating, informative, must-read for anyone interested in trading. As any trader knows, there is an emotional rollercoaster, and daily trials that need to be overcome, and Mike has successfully created an easy-to-follow guide that not only helps you develop the mindsets needed for success but also that will shave years off your learning curve."

—Bob Lotich,
Best-selling author of *Simple Money, Rich Life*

"The biggest misconception new traders have when learning how to trade is that their technical or fundamental strategy will be all they need to become a successful trader, but without the proper mindset, they will never find success as a trader. *The Trading Mindwheel* lays out eight essential skills that will be worth more to a trader than any technical or fundamental strategy they will learn."

—Anthony Crudele,
Futures Trader, Host of Futures Radio Show Podcast.

"Having been a trader and investor myself for many years and experienced many different market conditions, I fully accept that the ability to remain consistent and focused is essential. I have also realized that, at times, you can feel isolated and lonely. In the world of the Internet today, there is a sea of information, much of which is counterproductive to traders and investors. Quality resources are sparse. Even most successful traders keep their cards close to their chests. I want to thank Mike for writing this book because this is what traders and investors need. The quality of this book is the standard of tool that actually provides traders and investors with an edge. A must-read for anyone serious about making a success of trading."

—Jason Graystone,
Trader and Investor, Cofounder of Tier One Trading,
Host of *Always Free* Podcast

"Mike's book is a breath of fresh air in an otherwise suffocating world of trading education. No bells, whistles, or promises, simply an inside look at what it really takes to be a consistently profitable trader. Most books spend far too much time teaching "secret methods" or "magic strategies" that promise to bring results. This one takes a no-fluff approach and focuses on the key categories that need to be addressed if a trader wants to become and more importantly, remain successful."

—Akil Stokes,
Cofounder of Tier One Trading,
Host of *The Trading Coach* Podcast

"Michael goes *deep* on techniques, tactics, and self-analysis. In these areas, Michael *guides* us on how to use proven investing techniques and how to honestly do a good self-assessment on how to use the techniques and how to *improve your approach with the techniques*! Our best friend and our worst enemy greets us in the mirror each morning. The foundations given in Michael's book will help you realize your strengths, your weaknesses, and *how to be the best investor you can be*."

—Patrick Walker,
IBD Meetup Leader,
Founder of Mission Winners

The Trading Mindwheel

The Trading Mindwheel

Eight Essential Skills
for Trading Mastery

Michael Lamothe

WILEY

Published by John Wiley & Sons, Inc., Hoboken, New Jersey.
Published simultaneously in Canada.

For general information on our other products and services or for technical support, please contact our Customer Care Department within the United States at (800) 762-2974, outside the United States at (317) 572-3993 or fax (317) 572-4002.

Wiley also publishes its books in a variety of electronic formats. Some content that appears in print may not be available in electronic formats. For more information about Wiley products, visit our web site at www.wiley.com.

Library of Congress Cataloging-in-Publication Data

Names: Lamothe, Michael, author.
Title: The trading mindwheel : eight essential skills for trading mastery /
  Michael Lamothe.
Description: Hoboken, New Jersey : John Wiley & Sons, Inc., [2023] |
  Includes index.
Identifiers: LCCN 2022053836 (print) | LCCN 2022053837 (ebook) | ISBN
  9781119868248 (cloth) | ISBN 9781119868262 (adobe pdf) | ISBN
  9781119868255 (epub)
Subjects: LCSH: Stocks. | Stockbrokers.
Classification: LCC HG4661 .L356 2023 (print) | LCC HG4661 (ebook) | DDC
  332.63/22--dc23/eng/20230123
LC record available at https://lccn.loc.gov/2022053836
LC ebook record available at https://lccn.loc.gov/2022053837

Cover Design: Wiley
Cover Images: © pking4th/Getty Images, linear_design/Shutterstock, nexusby/Shutterstock, Alexander Lysenko/Shutterstock, mayrum/Shutterstock

Sometimes life sends us angels.
I've been blessed with two.
This book is dedicated to
my wife Melissa and my daughter Lily.

Table of Contents

Foreword – By Mark Minervini

Two-time U.S. Investing Champion

Several years ago, while traveling to New York City on business, I received a request from Michael Lamothe, asking me to meet with him. I agreed, and we got together at a local juice bar on Lexington Avenue. From that very first impression, I was struck by what a sincere, kind person he is, and immediately I took a liking to him. Since then, that initial impression has been confirmed, many times over. Today, I'm honored and proud to call Michael Lamothe a friend.

Over the years, I've watched Michael grow as a stock trader, a person, and a coach. He is truly motivated to help others. Now, in *The Trading Mindwheel*, he has brought that passion and motivation to fruition.

The Trading Mindwheel dives into essential areas of trading that are too often avoided: the psychology, the emotions, and other aspects that often go unnoticed and unmeasured. Most impressive, in this book Mike has done a great job of quantifying and delivering a systematic process for how to deal with the most pressing issues that most traders face daily: understanding the psychology and controlling the emotions that come with the risk and reward of trading.

From my own experience, and having written extensively about the importance of mindset, I can attest that emotions and psychology are what make or break anyone's success in any endeavor. In trading, you can have the best system that generates high-probability entry and exit points, but if you cannot master your emotions and your thinking, you will struggle. I know because I've seen it countless times with thousands of traders, and in my early days of trading I lived that challenge, too.

As I learned over four decades of trading, as well as in business, and competitive sports, success always comes down to how we think and what we believe. As I wrote in my own book, *Mindset Secrets for Winning: How to Bring Personal Power to Everything You Do* (Access Publishing, 2019): "Champions understand that hope is not a strategy. The best performers never trust greatness to chance. Instead, they actively create the conditions that allow them to be at their personal best. They decide to be winners, and they live each day with that goal in mind, because they recognize that when conditions are right, nature always fulfills its promise."

Michael takes this universal truth and applies it specifically and systematically to trading, with the wisdom that can only come from experience and the honesty that is derived from self-examination. He walks his talk on every page, sharing what he knows to be true for himself—and so many others.

I know from personal experience how much passion and work goes into writing a book. It involves far more time and energy than most authors ever get compensated for. The real reward comes from knowing how much you've helped others. And that's Michael's promise in *The Trading Mindwheel*.

In reading this book, you will come away with ideas, concepts, and tools that will help transform your thinking and your results. I highly recommend that you read this book—not just once, but several times. As with any great book, *The Trading Mindwheel* should not just be read, it should be studied.

There is no doubt that for Mike, writing this book was a labor of love.

For you, I hope reading it will be as well.

Introduction

Hi, this is Mike Lamothe. Thank you for taking the time to read *The Trading Mindwheel*. I hope you enjoy reading it as much as I enjoyed writing it. The process has been truly transformative for me.

The purpose of this book is not only to provide you with the basic framework for successful trading, the skills involved, and what it really takes, but also to show you how personal mindsets, psychology, and beliefs are interwoven into all aspects of trading. To drive this point home, I've decided to share with you some of my personal story—triumphs, failures, misfortunes, personal pain and suffering, and what it finally took to overcome those challenges and reach success.

What I've learned through the years is that at just about any juncture, things could have gone completely off the rails. Sometimes they did! However, unlike the movies, as long as we still have breath in our bodies, there isn't some absolute point of no return. There's *ALWAYS* a way for us to get back up, dust ourselves off, hit the refresh button, and carry on.

Enjoy the journey.

THE START OF SOMETHING LIFE CHANGING

It was June of 2018. We were gathered to celebrate my dad's 70th birthday. A small gathering of close family and friends at my dad's favorite restaurant in Port Jefferson, New York, the Lobster House. After we ordered some appetizers and a round of drinks, with my three-year-old daughter, Lily, squirming in my arms, I held up a beer from a local brewery, took a deep breath, and stood up to say the following words:

> *Even now this is challenging to say ... Dad, more than 30 years ago you rescued me from what could have turned out to be a really, really terrible life. You are my hero.*

A few years ago I read this book called Your One Word *by Evan Carmichael. The idea he had was that there's one word that acts as your guiding light. Your north star, so to speak, and I discovered that my one word was "Inspire." There were a few exercises in the book that led me to pick "Inspire," but until recently I didn't fully understand why. I've now come to realize that it came from you!*

A big part of this "one word" concept was developing a credo. Three other words help you define your one word. I chose "Believe," "Perseverance," and "Love." Again, I was doing the exercises but not fully comprehending what led me to select those three words. And then, it dawned on me. . . .

Throughout my life, Dad, you've always believed in me even when I didn't believe in you or in myself. When you and Mom divorced all those years ago and I came to live with you, it was hard. I was told many negative things about you, and back then I believed them all. I struggled with those negative beliefs for the first ten years we lived together. Perhaps you were able to tell I was struggling by my words and my actions. But despite all that, you never stopped trying, and you never stopped believing in me. For a decade you persevered to be the best dad you could be, not knowing if I would ever realize how hard you were working or even show you an ounce of love in return. You showed me so much love for so long that I just had to tell you this—you're my hero, and you're the person who has made me want to inspire others. And I know I don't tell you this enough, but I love you.

Less than a year later my father died of a sudden heart attack. As much as it pained me to lose him, I was at peace because I had told him what I needed to say. I was filled with so much gratitude that I got to say what I wanted to say to him before he passed. So grateful that I didn't leave those words on the table. **What I said in that speech I would never have said if I hadn't put in the work to understand my beliefs,** where they came from, to shift my perspective, and to view what was once anger, guilt, and sadness from a traumatic childhood to now be important teachers. To understand that where we start out doesn't have to be where we finish. To understand that we have the capacity to begin these shifts in a heartbeat.

The most important things between us were said. He knew how I felt. He knew everything he struggled through meant something. And even as I sit here and type this it brings a tear to my eyes . . . and that's the thing—that's the important thing. Life and all of its experiences can serve us *if we allow them to*. It may not seem like it in the moment, but even the harshest, most painful things in life can serve us. It's crazy how small actions such as reading a book and doing the suggested exercises can lead to results far greater than we could ever dream of.

You may be saying to yourself, "That's an incredible story, but what does this have to do with trading?" Well, I'm glad you asked because the answer is *EVERYTHING*. It has everything to do with trading!

I decided to write *The Trading Mindwheel* because it is our beliefs that can either help us or hinder us with whatever it is that we wish for. Be it the ability to openly express our feelings, overcome childhood trauma, build a fortune, live a happy and fulfilled life, or simply trade better. I find it helpful to think of beliefs as you might an operating system in a computer.

Imagine, if you will, that you are getting ready to place a trade. You sit down at your computer, turn it on, and wait for it to boot. It takes a few minutes. but this is okay and totally normal to you. You're used to it. After all, this machine has served you well for the last 20 years, and as they say, "If it ain't broke, don't fix it," right? It's been trusty, reliable, and comfortable, and you're used to it.

Sounds ridiculous, right? Who is still using the same computer from 20 years ago? But what if I told you that this is what most of us do with our belief systems? We continue to run the same old programming from 20 years ago. Perhaps it's time we take a look around and consider an upgrade!

This book is designed to help you discover and install many of the upgrades needed for successful trading. It will help you question and challenge the status quo. It will introduce you to the building blocks needed to lay the foundation for your successful trading future. We all need upgrades from time to time, myself included. The sooner we can admit that to ourselves, the sooner we can begin the process. If we're truly honest with ourselves about where we're at, it makes figuring out the path of how to get to where we want to go a lot easier.

Throughout this book, you will encounter many exercises. Just like my first book, *The MARA Mindshift Guide: A Trading Beliefs Workbook*, if you want to get the most out of this book, you must do the exercises. Skim through this book, and you'll still get value, but you'll be leaving a lot on the table.

Some simple coffee table wisdom my dad used to give me all the time was, "Always do your best." Has anyone ever told you that? It's simple advice, but how often do we find ourselves doing less than our best? Here's another question, How often do we find ourselves attempting to do more than our best? I don't know about you, but I've found myself on either side of that coin multiple times in my life. Funny enough, I've found it to be like a balancing act and one often leading to the other. Doing less than we're capable of and then scrambling to make up for the lost time, being gung ho for something new and exciting, rushing in without much of a plan or the wrong expectations, attempting to take on everything at once, and quickly becoming overwhelmed. Have you felt this way?

To stay on track, perform at our best, and achieve the results we're after, I find it best to:

1. Develop clear goals;
2. Develop plans to meet those goals; and
3. Focus doggedly on consistent execution of those plans toward those goals.

We'll discuss each of these—goal setting, plan development, and execution—in detail in later chapters. For now, think of goals as you would think of putting an address into a GPS. The more specific we are, the easier it will be for us to get from where we are to where we want to go. With clear goals, even when life puts up roadblocks and we get knocked off track, we can still find our way over, around, or through to get back on track.

You may find some of the exercises in this book to be easy, some of them hard, some of them quick, and some may take a while. All of that is okay. All of that is part of the journey. What I promise you is that it will all be worth it, and your efforts will be well rewarded in ways you may never have imagined.

In this book, we're going to leave no stone left unturned. I'm going to share with you everything that has led to my personal success and the success of the thousands of traders I've coached and mentored through the years. I'm going to share with you the ongoing efforts, strategies, and tactics we use for continuous improvement.

Maintaining success that lasts takes a certain level of tenacity and perseverance. I believe that we're all capable of this. That we all have it within us. And even if you're reading this and you're at a point where you're questioning if that fire within you has gone out, I'm here to let you know that it can always be rekindled, relit, stoked—and it can grow!

While this book shares much of my story, this book really isn't about me. It's about you. It's about your journey. It's about the things that will help you achieve the levels of trading success that you are after and beyond.

The stories in this book are meant to inspire, offer a fresh perspective, help you avoid errors and traps. Learn not only what really works but why it works. At the time of this writing, I have traded for over 20 years. My first account was opened in the summer of 1999. Since then I have made more mistakes than I thought existed. I've suffered several blown accounts. I even swore that I'd give up trading entirely, *twice*—and nearly did! In fact, if we could go back in time and talk to my younger self, I'm sure he'd fall on the floor when we tell him that not only did we finally make it, but here we are writing a book and helping others achieve their dreams.

Yes, my friend, where we start out does not need to be where we finish. We all begin life as tiny specks that rapidly grow. That growth does not need to end after adolescence. It does, however, change from being something that happens automatically to becoming a choice.

We can choose to continue growing—growing our knowledge, health and well-being, wealth, wisdom, and influence, or we can choose not to. It's an individual choice, and there is no right or wrong answer. However, the question I often find myself asking is, Why not? Why not continue growing and becoming all that we can? We're only here for a short while after all. When we near the end of our lives, would we be satisfied with ourselves if we're unable to positively answer the question, Did I do my best?

Now before we continue, let's come up with some definitions of success and failure. Think of it as your first exercise in this book. So go ahead, put down the book, and grab some paper and something to write with.

Are you ready? Okay, great.

First, take a moment and think about the ways in which you define success. Write them down. You may already have a few ways that you've been defining success, and that's okay. Write whatever comes to mind about success. Ready? Go!

After you've written down what success means to you, answer the following questions.

- Does it have to do with achievement?
- Does it have to do with the process?
- Does it have to do with the outcomes?
- Is it something large?
- Is it grandiose?
- Is it something small?

It really helps to get these ideas out on paper. Trust me on this one. I used to be the person who would read a statement like that and think, "Yeah, sure," answer the questions in my head for a brief moment, and move right along. My results in trading, health, physical performance, family, and life, in general, all improved substantially and shockingly fast when I began writing. So if you haven't done so already, give it a shot! What do you have to lose? If you don't have paper and something to write with, type on your phone, tablet, or computer. If you can't write them now, do so as soon as you're able. You'll get infinitely more from it this way, I promise you.

Now that you've successfully done that, think of the ways in which you define failure. Write them down.

- What comes to mind when you think of failure?
- Is it outcome-based?
- What emotions do you associate with failure?

If your answers have something to do with achievement or outcomes, you're not alone. Most people look at success like this: "If I do _____ and achieve _____ outcome, then I was successful at _____. However, if I do _____ and do not achieve _____ outcome, then I was not successful at _____." While this may be straightforward and sound completely logical, there are some major flaws with this view of success when it comes to trading.

Simon Sinek, speaker, and best-selling author of *Start With Why*, shares that the problem with defining success based on outcomes is that it's too shortsighted. For example, if we go to the gym and afterward look at ourselves in the mirror, we won't see any results. Do this again a few days in a row, and we'll conclude that it doesn't work because we don't see any results. However, we know that through consistent effort we will achieve success, even though we may not know the exact day that happens.

Trading is a game of probabilities. Many of the best traders in the world such as recent US Investing Champions Mark Minervini, Oliver Kell, and Leif Soreide, each with annual returns well into the triple digits, have win rates near 50%!

In trading, if we were to judge success based solely on the outcomes of individual trades, we may have taken a snapshot of these champions at some point in time and considered them failures! It's the wrong perspective! I mean, most of us would be quite satisfied with triple-digit annual returns. Wouldn't you?

I think we can come up with a better definition of success. However, before we do, let's dispel the individual outcome definition further. Here's a question to help. Where does defining success based on individual outcomes tend to lead?

More often than not, those who experience "system hopping," the act of jumping from system to system or frequently changing trading styles or rules, define success and failure based on the results of individual trades and/or small, non–statistically significant groups of trades.

For example, suppose you learned a trading system and after 30 trades you were sitting at a net loss. Would it be time to switch systems or styles completely? Maybe, but maybe not! In most cases, to achieve a level of statistical significance where we can spot a true pattern versus random chance, we'd want to see at least 100 trades.

If the thought of trading a system 100 times to find out whether it works or not scares you, do not worry. When we get to the chapter on testing, we'll discuss how you can find reliable results faster with little to no additional money out of pocket required.

Back to our definition of success: If we're not defining our success based on outcomes alone, what should we define our success on? I suggest part of our definition be based on our level of progress, effort, and following the process.

Here's a quick story to help illustrate the point.

The Parable of the Sower and the Seed

Behold, a sower went out to sow. And as he sowed, some seed fell by the wayside; and the birds came and devoured them. Some fell on stony places, where they did not have much earth; they immediately sprang up because they had no depth of earth. But when the sun was up they were scorched, and because they had no root they withered away. And some fell among thorns, and the thorns sprang up and choked them. But others fell on good ground and yielded a crop, some a hundred-fold, some sixty, some thirty.

You may look at this parable and conclude that the moral of the story is that our job as the sower is to simply sow, keep on sowing no matter what, and eventually good things will happen. This may be part of the answer, but it certainly isn't all of it. It took me nearly a decade of trying this out with the market to realize this.

While consistent effort is a major part of success and we should acknowledge it, it isn't everything. For example, the sower must have had at least some basic knowledge of how to sow, right? At least enough to not dump all of the seeds in a pile in the middle of the field and walk away. Certainly enough to not overanalyze each spot where he or she was going to sow, lest not enough seed would get sowed and there wouldn't be enough crops! And perhaps the sower knew enough to follow the process of sowing and allow the systems of nature and numbers to take over. Couldn't something similar be said about trading?

Here's a question worth asking: Could the sower's sowing be improved? Absolutely! The sower could get a better bag so that less seed fell by the wayside. He could have better knowledge of where the good soil is and how to avoid the stony or thorny places. Yes, the sower's skills can be improved, and our trading skills can be improved, too. In order to do so, we need to focus on the process first. Focus on the basics first and more advanced skills later. Have faith that following the process will yield the results we're after. If we work to improve our skills, we can grow, come back, grow some more, and become the best we're capable of being.

So what are the essential skills required for trading? What are the skills that will really help us roll faster down the path of trading success? I'm glad you asked. Allow me to introduce you to "The Trading Mindwheel."

PHILOSOPHY OF THE TRADING MINDWHEEL

What is the trading "mindwheel"?

Think of it like this. Picture a bicycle. Think of one that you'd consider reliable and would trust to ride on a warm summer's day through the park for a good time. What condition is this bike in? Picture the wheels. What do they look like? How about the tires? Are they new? Fully inflated? Of course they are, right? The bicycle you just pictured is the type of bicycle we're going to create for your trading with the trading mindwheel.

Each of the skills needed to trade successfully is a spoke on the wheel. At the center of the wheel, the axle, are our beliefs. Our beliefs hold everything else together. In fact, let's think about it for a moment.

What are some of the most negative beliefs you've heard about trading? Perhaps you've heard that the markets are rigged and that unless you have scores of analysts working for you around the clock, you really don't stand a chance at being successful. Could you imagine someone rolling down the path of trading success with beliefs like that? Of course not, right?

If any of that sounds like you, don't worry. I have some good news for you. Because we have the freedom of choice, we can choose which beliefs we hold, which we adopt, and which we let go of. In later chapters, we'll discuss how to do this.

Unfortunately, when it comes to trading, most of us just hop on the bike and start pedaling. Some of us may even expect the trading equivalent of winning the Tour de France within our first few times out. This usually doesn't work out too well.

More often than not, what happens when we approach trading this way is we either fail right out of the gate, or, worse, we have a big winning trade that inflates our ego!

As time goes by we realize trading is far more challenging than we had initially thought. We do not come close to our idea of "winning." Instead, we struggle fall, skin our knees, and likely crash into a bush.

It's at this point that we start to wonder about what went wrong. The earlier thoughts of the market being rigged and us needing scores of analysts in order to win start to creep back in. Meanwhile, we totally forgot that not only did we not inspect the bike before we hopped on, but we also failed to notice that it was rusted, had a set of square wheels, and half-inflated tires. If we're being totally honest with ourselves, was it really the "market's fault" that we struggled, fell, and skinned our knees?

We've all blamed someone or something else at some point in our lives. But what has that really gotten us? If we're honest with ourselves, maybe it felt good to offload that blame in the moment. But where have pointing fingers, passing the buck, and playing the blame game really gotten us in the end?

Playing the blame game in the past does not preclude us from success in the future. However, if we want positive change, the blame game needs to end now. That is, of course, presuming that you want to ride down the path of success. If you do, a rusted bike with square wheels won't get the job done.

So what exactly is the "Trading Mindwheel," and what are the skills needed to trade successfully?

I've boiled it down to eight essential trading skills that are requirements for success. If any of the eight is missing or underdeveloped, adding or improving in these areas will be your quickest path to success. I've drawn these conclusions after more than 20 years of experience and research. This includes both primary research consisting of my own hypotheses, testing, trial and error, and results, as well as secondary research including studying some of the best traders, investors, coaches, and psychologists living and deceased. These titans include, but are not limited to, William O'Neil, Nicolas Darvas, Jesse Livermore, Stan Weinstein, Van Tharp, Mark Minervini, David Ryan, Ed Seykota, Ray Dalio, Mark Douglas, Alexander Elder, Brett

Steenbarger, Jim Roppel, and Tony Robbins. It's great to have aspirational mentors. I'm extremely blessed to have not only worked with a few of the aforementioned people but to have become friends with them.

The Eight Essential Skills Needed for Successful Trading Include:

1. MINDSET: Beliefs, Belief Systems, Emotions, and Habits;
2. JOURNALING: Step One of Accountability and Continuous Improvement;
3. ANALYSIS: Analyzing Trades and Markets;
4. RISK: Initial Capital Risk, Position Sizing, Potential Reward;
5. TRADE MANAGEMENT: Managing Risk throughout the life of the trade;
6. PORTFOLIO MANAGEMENT: The BIG Picture and Assessing Our Total Risk;
7. POST ANALYSIS: Step Two of Continuous Improvement;
8. TESTING: Factor Modeling, Back Testing, and Forward-Testing.

Here's a little prelude of each part of the mindwheel before we get into the heart of each in greater detail within this book.

MINDSET: Beliefs, Belief Systems, Emotions, and Habits

Mindset covers more than you might think. For the sake of this book, mindset includes our beliefs, belief systems, emotions, habits, and general market psychology. So while it does have its own set of chapters, the mindset theme will be recurring throughout the entire book.

Mindset is at the center of the mindwheel and for good reason. We have beliefs about everything. Over time these beliefs become interconnected and can form systems. The belief systems form the stories we tell ourselves. These stories guide our actions for better or worse. So if you ever hear the term "BS," it may just be referring to a **B**elief **S**ystem.

The truth is that all of our BS for better or worse, has served us at some point in our lives. What happens, however, is that most of us don't revisit our old BS. We just shovel new BS on top of the old. What we end up with is a confusing stinky pile where things don't grow so well.

All kidding aside, the first steps we'll take together will be revisiting our old belief systems and seeing what's there. We will question how these belief systems served us in the past. We'll figure out what our goals are now. And then we'll ask ourselves if our current set of beliefs are leading us closer to, or further from, our goals. We'll reconcile them and install new, upgraded beliefs that will allow us to grow into our goals.

 ## JOURNALING: Step One of Accountability and Continuous Improvement

It's often said that the market is the best teacher. Well, if we believe this to be true, then we better take good notes! In fact, one of the most common factors I've observed among traders who succeed versus the ones that don't is journaling!

To their detriment, I've seen many new and aspiring traders brush journaling aside, considering it a chore at best or a waste of time at worst. They'll "try" journaling, often giving it a half-hearted effort. Often they will then repeat the same mistakes again and again for months or even years while being completely oblivious to the reasons why.

Peter Drucker, the famous business consultant, famously said, "What gets measured, gets managed." There's a lot of truth in that. Journaling is an important first step in the measurement process. After all, we can't measure nor can we manage what we don't have, can we?

We'll discuss the types of data, thoughts, and emotions we'll want to capture in our journals. We'll even discuss the various types of journals that exist, the specific data points we should strongly consider capturing, as well as the strategies and tactics involving when and how to capture them, and of course the reasons why. But for now, please understand that the most important thing with journaling is that we simply get started. Yes, this means that in the beginning, it will likely be a little messy, perhaps a tad unorganized, and we may even have to deal with a bit of uncertainty about whether we're overdoing it or underdoing it. Rest assured that all of that is okay and is actually a part of the process. Our journals will evolve with us. The only way this evolution begins is to get started.

Again, it's easy to get bogged down in the details, feel overwhelmed, and put it off. This is why the emphasis is on getting started and keeping the momentum going (and we'll discuss tactics for keeping the momentum going too).

ANALYSIS: Analyzing Trades and Markets

When we think of analysis, many things may come to mind. We can analyze individual trades and investments. We can go broader and analyze markets and global macro events. If you've ever read Jack Schwager's *Market Wizards* book series (if you haven't, then I highly recommend it), you already know that there are all sorts of successful methods of analyzing markets and trades. For the purposes of this book, we'll discuss the various types of analysis I've tried, the pitfalls, the successes, and perhaps most importantly, the whys behind them all.

RISK: Initial Capital Risk, Position Sizing, Potential Reward

There are lots of ways to think about risk. For the purposes of this book, we'll be focused on risk as it directly affects our accounts. I'm talking about the capital at risk if we lose on a trade or investment, the size of the position we'll be taking on relative to our account size, as well as the potential rewards we hope to receive in relation to the risk we're taking on. We'll break down some relatively simple ways to understand and calculate risk and provide you with some free tools to help you calculate it quickly.

TRADE MANAGEMENT: Managing Risk throughout the Life of the Trade

Once a trade or investment is executed, its management begins. We'll want to lay the groundwork for our trade management well in advance. A few of the questions we'll ask ourselves include: What rules will we follow? What types of signals will we look for to add or reduce? When will we look for these signals? Daily? Weekly? Longer or shorter?

While trades and investments are indeed managed in real time, it does not mean that we should fly by the seat of our pants. In fact, many of the fears you've likely heard of and perhaps experienced, such as fear of loss or fear of being wrong, are commonly linked to a lack of preparation and a rock-solid plan.

We'll discuss various management techniques, from active to passive and everything in between, from what's worked best for me, for my clients, and why, and how it can evolve over time.

PORTFOLIO MANAGEMENT: The BIG Picture and Assessing Our Total Risk

Managing individual trades and investments is important. However, to roll down the path of trading success, we must think bigger. We must consider how we'll manage trades in relation to one another, to changing market conditions, and to the larger whole of the various asset classes we may own.

To go back to our sower example from earlier, we must determine which seeds we'll plant where and how much, how we'll space them out, during which periods we'll plant, and what happens if we get more or fewer crops than expected. In a nutshell, that is portfolio management.

Another idea that we're after here is balance. Balance comes in a variety of flavors. Some things we'll consider are how our portfolio is weighted in terms of groups and sectors, how it's weighted among asset classes, and how much total risk we're taking on at any given time. For example, when the market is hot and everything seems to be working in our favor, it's quite possible to get heavy (putting on several trades at once) in a hurry. Knowing our total risk becomes even more important. The market may be hot, but we don't want to get burned. If the market has a sudden move against us, awareness of and managing our total risk saves us from getting scorched.

POST ANALYSIS: Step Two of Continuous Improvement

A simple way we can begin to think about post analysis is the act of looking back at our work and figuring out what went right, what went wrong, and how we can improve. It's pretty clear then that post analysis and journaling go hand in hand, isn't it? Without some form of journaling, we'd have nothing to post-analyze. Without post analysis, we'd be stuck where we are, making little progress, and perhaps feeling that we're running around in circles. If you've ever felt confused about your trading, have felt that you've plateaued, or worse, are heading in the wrong direction, post analysis can be a major part of the solution. When we get to the chapters on post analysis we'll discuss strategies, tactics, tools, and intervals for doing it well and ways to remain consistent with it.

TESTING: Factor Modeling, Back Testing, and Forward Testing

Of the eight essential trading skills, this one seems to get the most overlooked. For years I was guilty of it too. In fact, I used to see it as both a useless waste of time and a major pain in the behind. As my friend and fellow author Adam Sarhan kindly pointed out long ago, this was a blind spot.

My belief at the time was, "If other legendary traders like Jesse Livermore, Nicolas Darvas, William O'Neil, and Mark Minervini (some of my biggest influences), have thoroughly tested their systems and their systems not only work but made their fortunes, why should I bother testing them? I'll just do exactly what they did and run with it."

Have you ever fallen into this line of thinking? I'll tell you from experience that unfortunately, this is a shortcut that only gets us halfway to our destination. We end up crudely performing a type of forward testing. Because we've taken shortcuts, we lack the proper framework to make steady progress with our new system. Instead, we end up needing to double back and spend double the amount of time and effort we would have needed if we had only just followed the process from the beginning.

So when I initially tried, failed, and tried again, rather than feeling that I was making small, incremental progress, and getting somewhere, I often felt like a loser! Yes, how we frame things is important too, and it ties right into mindset.

We'll get into forward testing and effective ways to do it in later chapters but for now, think of it as having an idea and testing it in real time.

Without knowing it, by taking the ideas I had read about in books and attempting to trade off them, in a sense I was forward testing.

Was this a great test? Hardly! I wasn't tracking anything unless you count staring at my profits and losses with bloodshot eyes as "tracking."

If I was profitable, I told myself that the system was working. If not, something was wrong, either with me, the system, the market, or something else. These beliefs had me running around in circles unaware that I had concocted a recipe for heartache and disaster.

Done well and with intention, factor modeling and testing can save us a great deal of time, effort, and money.

Are you beginning to see how each of the spokes of the mindwheel are belief driven? It's for this reason that mindset is the axle and at the center of the mindwheel and why we'll be discussing it in the next chapter.

One Note before We Start

It's very tempting to see a book with "Eight Essential Skills" in the title and want to jump straight to the ones you think you need the most help with. I totally get that and have felt similarly when I was in your shoes. Know that each section of this book builds on the last. You'll have a far greater and far deeper understanding of the material if you read it in its entirety in the order presented first. After you've gone through it once, then feel free to hop around.

Congratulations on getting started. This already puts you ahead of most. Let's begin!

MINDSET: Beliefs, Belief Systems, Emotions, and Habits

It all starts here.

Mindset is the epicenter and the axle of the Trading Mindwheel. It is that from which everything else is interconnected and flows. Fortunes have been made and lost through the years because of mindset. When we talk about mindset, we're talking about our beliefs, belief systems, emotions, and even habits.

One of the most famous, most extreme, and unfortunately most tragic examples of both what mindset is capable of doing for us as traders and investors as well as what can happen when it goes off the rails comes from that of Jesse Livermore.

JESSE LIVERMORE'S STORY

Jesse's unique style of trading enabled him to not only compound and build a massive fortune but to become one of the richest people in the world at the time. Starting at only 14 years of age in 1891, he bet $5 on Chicago, Burlington, and Quincy Railroad at a bucket shop (a place that took leveraged bets on stock prices but didn't buy or sell the actual stock). On this bet he made about 60%, turning his $5 into $8.12.

He continued to do this for a couple of years, and by the age of 16, he was regularly bringing home about $200 per week. A few more years went by, and at age 23, he was able to move to New York. Soon after, he made an incredible trade at Harris, Hutton & Company stockbrokers, turning $10,000 into $50,000 in only five days! And then came his first blowup. He anticipated a correction, went short using 400% margin, and lost it all.

Not to be deterred, Jesse borrowed some money, moved to St. Louis (where no one knew him), and started betting in bucket shops again. Later that same year, he bought stock in Northern Pacific Railway and parlayed $10,000 into $500,000!

This type of back-and-forth of extremely massive wins and eventual blowups continued for Jesse. He had to declare bankruptcy multiple times throughout his life. He had a trading system and a set of rules that enabled him to not only win but to become one of the wealthiest people in the world. Unfortunately, as author Stephen Covey once wrote, "Nothing fails like success." After Jesse's massive wins and getting back on top, he'd eventually rest on his laurels, get sloppy, and stop following the rules that had enabled him to amass his fortune.

Wild swings from extreme wealth (over $100 million in 1929, which today would be equal to approximately $1.6 billion) to needing to declare bankruptcy multiple times eventually drove Jesse mad. He fell into a deep depression and in 1940, he committed suicide.

MINDSET IS EVERYTHING

The emotional highs and lows of this game are real. It can leave us with a feeling of being on top of the highest mountain, at the bottom of the lowest cavern, and everywhere in between.

If we can get our mindset right, we'll not only be *way* ahead of the game, but everything else will have a much stronger ability to flow. If we don't . . . well, if Jesse's story wasn't enough, could you imagine riding a bike or driving a car with the center of its wheels being compromised? I don't think we'd get very far. I don't think it would end well either. Do you? The same applies to trading.

As Socrates famously said, "Know thyself."

Our beliefs and belief systems provide the framework for how we view and interact with the world. Therefore, it's imperative that we not only become intimately familiar with each but also that we actively manage, grow, and shape each. In fact, the greater our understanding of beliefs and belief systems, the greater our empathy and emotional intelligence will become. From here, things like general trading psychology and market psychology will start making a lot more sense. We'll be able to grow easier and faster in the other areas of the trading mindwheel as well. We'll develop our innate but rarely awakened skill to objectively view things (in this case trades and investments) from multiple angles: buy side, sell side, and as a neutral observer. Eventually, this skill may even become second nature and near effortless for us, akin to breathing.

So much is entrenched in this area of mindset that it behooves us to start from the very beginning. By "very beginning" I mean going back as far as we can remember. Yes, I'm talking about our early childhoods. Our early childhood is where our beliefs and belief systems began to develop.

TAKING INVENTORY OF OUR BELIEFS

What beliefs do you have? Where did they come from? In what ways have they served you in the past and in what ways are they attempting to serve you now?

ALL of the beliefs we have are attempting to serve us in some way.

If you're skeptical of that last sentence, don't worry. I was too. I had thought that some beliefs were good, some were bad, some were empowering, and others were deliberately attempting to hold me back.

My stance shifted when I realized I was judging the beliefs based on the outcomes they were currently producing, not on what they had produced in the past or on how I was using them in the present.

Think of it like this. When you buy a new computer, it comes with software. It all works fairly well together and gets the job done. A few years go by. Now when you run the computer it feels a bit slower. It's not working quite as well as when you took it out of the box. If you didn't make any updates to the hardware or software, you would likely conclude that the slowdown is completely natural. In this case, you'd be right! Slowing down is natural *IF* you don't make any upgrades!

Our beliefs are just like that computer. When we first got them they were serving us well. They are still attempting to serve us now. We just need to go into our mental operating systems, take a look around, and make some updates.

This is no easy task. For most of us, digging into our beliefs and belief systems represents a major undertaking. At times it might feel like rolling a boulder up a steep hill. At least that's how I felt the first time I did this. There's a great deal of work involved.

Taking inventory of what we believe involves digging up the past. When we dig up the past, it's inevitable that there will be a few skeletons that we find. We may not like some of them. Some of them may scare us. Others we may regret. We may even find a few past wounds that still need healing. No, this task won't be an easy one. But growth is seldom easy.

I'll share with you a brief story of one of the wounds I unearthed during this exercise. Had I not done this exercise, the wound would likely still be festering to this day. Unbeknownst to me at the time, it was not only impacting my trading, but it was also impacting many other areas of my life as well.

2 A.M. WAKEUP CALL

It was 2 a.m. when I was jostled awake. For some reason, that time is etched in my memory. It took me a second to realize where I was since I knew this wasn't home. The old, yellowed wallpaper peeling off the walls, the musky scent of mildew, and the old rabbit-eared antennae television set still on— the ominous bleep and rainbow bars on the screen startling me as I awoke from that place between dreams and reality.

This wasn't my home. It wasn't my room with my transformers lining the shelves, my beloved Optimus Prime under my bed, and G.I. Joes sprawled across the floor. Nothing about this seedy motel room resembled anything of the home I knew. My toys were gone . . . Optimus Prime disappeared in the shuffle as we packed out of our home, and it all felt like some nightmare I kept praying would end.

But this was my reality: I was a six-year-old boy who was homeless. There was no going home.

As my eyes blinked open, I still wished I would wake up and my mom and dad would be living together again in our house in Centereach, with Joey, our poodle. I always remember Joey being so big. In reality, he was barely three feet tall when standing on his hind legs. Everything looks bigger when you're a kid, you know? Anyway, Joey was gone now. And so was the comfortable life with my mom and dad—that reverie of going to drive-in movies and sitting on the roof of the car, with only the stars and the huge movie screen lighting the night. All of that disappeared in an instant like the projector crapping out on you once the movie started getting good.

I was too young to remember all of the details, but my parents went through a messy divorce. A year or two later my mom remarried and had sole custody of me. I lived with my mom and stepdad in Centereach, Long Island, and my father was starting a new life in his hometown of Astoria, Queens.

I was told many things about my father. I was told that he was a drunk and that he didn't care about me. That he hid his drinking money in his shoe and urinated in my crib when I was a baby.

Messed up, right?

Was any of this really true? Well, true or not, as a vulnerable child just starting the first grade, I believed what I was told. I had little reason not to. I trusted my mom and stepdad. So, thanks to these beliefs that I was gifted, accepted, and didn't question, I both despised and feared my father.

Life is complex, and when I look back on those early years, there were still instances of good times. . . . Like my stepfather teaching me how to ride a bike, playing laser tag with him and my mom in the backyard, starting grade school and meeting some friends.

Then, somewhere in the midst of my early childhood, my mom and step-dad's finances took a turn for the worse. She wasn't working. He lost his job. And soon we were evicted from our home. For a few months, we were living in and out of sketchy motel rooms.

I knew this wasn't normal. I knew this was unfair.

I thought back to when I was playing in my bedroom with Optimus Prime, my hero back then. They made a *Transformers* movie, and within the first few scenes Optimus wasn't just killed off. He was completely obliterated in as gory a fashion as a cartoon robot could be. I was so devastated that I actually set up a funeral for him and "buried" my hero in a shoebox under my bed.

At this point, even my hero was gone, along with so many things I thought were stable in my life. I began to learn early on and in a very real way that everything is temporary, could die, and be gone forever. Even still, I could hear Optimus Prime's voice in the animated cartoon with his thunderous rallying call, "Transform and Roll Out." Like he was calling out to me not to crumble. That even heroes need to rise again.

My mom's voice tickled my ear as my eyes adjusted to the darkness.

"Mikey," she whispered, "you need to get up."

I rubbed my eyes, her words not computing. "Why?" I asked.

She took an uneasy breath, stealing a glance at my stepdad. "We can't do this anymore. Your dad is coming to pick you up. You're going to live with him now."

I don't remember much else from that night more than 35 years ago. But I remember that crippling and frantic fear of being forced to leave my mom. I didn't want to leave her. I fought. I yelled. I screamed that I didn't want to leave. Living in a seedy motel in a sketchy part of town . . . I didn't care. I just wanted to stay with my mom.

My screams were futile. The decision had already been made. Why at 2 a.m. on some random night is anyone's guess. Maybe they were getting kicked out of that motel the following day. Maybe my mom realized she couldn't keep doing this to me. Whatever the reason, I packed up my clothes and waited, crying as my dad pulled up in his old Honda Accord. I wiped away tears, knowing I lost the battle.

As I started to leave, I don't remember hugging my mom, stepdad, or half-brother James. I don't remember what they said to me that night. I just remember getting into the car, watching through the window as the motel sign's flickering fluorescent lights faded in the distance as my dad and I drove along in silence on the empty road. I slept for most of the two-hour drive back to Astoria . . . for one moment at peace though my whole world felt like it was falling apart. My mom had just handed me over to live with what she had taught me to believe was a monster.

DECONSTRUCTING BELIEFS AND BELIEF SYSTEMS

Crazy story, right? Little did I know, but that trauma, the beliefs, the emotions, and the mindsets from it would haunt me for years. Not just during my childhood but through my teenage years and later into my early adult life.

It impacted my relationships with other people, money, and yes, trading. The deepest impact, however, was in my relationship with myself. And therein lies the blind spot that so many of us face. The thing that so often keeps us stuck while replaying the same stories and repeating the same mistakes over and over again.

Belief systems can sometimes act like a spiral with one belief building upon the next. For example, a belief of having little self-worth may spawn another belief that we're not worthy of love, success, financial well-being, etc. These beliefs can then turn into actions, and it becomes a self-fulfilling prophecy.

Beliefs like these can live deep in our subconscious. We may not even consciously realize their existence. Though if they are there, you'd better believe we can feel their ramifications.

For example, take an activity like trading. If a number of negative and limiting beliefs are running deep in our subconscious, they can later turn into self-sabotaging actions.

Trading can be relatively simple, straightforward, and with proper skill development, highly lucrative. When a host of negative and limiting beliefs are running in the background such as being worth little, not being worthy of love, or any kind of success, is it any wonder that self-sabotaging behavior is the result? Random trades. Not following carefully designed trading plans. Betting way too big, like Jesse Livermore. All of these behaviors are the result of negative and limiting beliefs.

Underlying trauma like this can be so debilitating that even attaining world-class status at the other seven essential trading skills won't be enough and will eventually lead to self-sabotaging behavior.

Mindset is the epicenter. Mindset holds everything else together.

Are the other seven essential skills important? Absolutely (we wouldn't include them in this book if they weren't)! But if we find that we've fallen into a pattern of self-sabotage, it's often a mindset-related issue. A core human need that we all have is to act in accordance with our own beliefs.

Want to upgrade results? Upgrade beliefs.

Our beliefs and belief systems are meant to serve us, not the other way around.

Let's go back to our example of how mindset acts as our internal operating system. If we have a negative operating system, how likely is it to produce positive results? Not much, right? Probably about the same likelihood of an apple tree producing oranges. Thankfully, we don't have to accept this when it comes to our mindset. We've been given the graces of change and the freedom of choice.

So how do we facilitate this change? It starts with awareness.

Awareness

If we want to positively change our beliefs, the first thing we need to do is become aware of them. It's my belief that lack of awareness is the thing holding most of us back.

Here's one more example to drive the point home even further. Picture your favorite small plant. It's pristine in every possible way. You were given this plant from someone who truly cares about you and loves you. It's springtime, and this plant is meant to be planted in a garden outside.

What's your next step?

Even if you don't have a "green thumb" I'm sure you wouldn't just leave the plant in the middle of the yard and hope for the best. No, you'd likely find a relatively clear spot where your plant would get the proper amount of sunlight and water it needs to thrive. You would then remove any weeds from the surrounding area, dig a hole, and then plant your new, pristine plant in a loving and caring way.

Beliefs can be very similar in this regard. We can purchase the best books and courses the world has to offer about trading. In these books there are world-class beliefs that when adopted, integrated, and acted upon will yield fortunes. However, if we leave them on the shelf with little to no action, it's the equivalent of leaving our new plant in the middle of the yard and hoping for the best.

Reading books and taking courses without an awareness of our beliefs won't get us very far either. This is the mistake that I made and many others have made as well. This is the mental equivalent of digging a hole and planting our new plant in a field full of weeds. How can we expect our beautiful new plant to grow and reach its full potential if we haven't weeded the garden first?

It took me a full decade to realize I was planting knowledge into a weed-filled garden. I struggled mightily and far more than necessary during this period. So before we go any further, let's take some time here and begin the weeding process.

Awareness Exercise 1

When it comes to trading, there are three sets of beliefs we'll want to become intimately familiar with. These include:

1. Our beliefs about Trading;
2. Our beliefs about Money;
3. Our beliefs about Ourselves.

We'll start with a writing exercise. You can begin this exercise now or later. Either way, know that this is an ongoing process. Self-development and self-mastery does not end. I repeat, self-development and self-mastery *Does Not End*! You will experience many aha moments along the way.

No one steps in the same river twice, for it's not the same river and you're not the same person.

—Heraclitus, Philosopher

This exercise should be performed separately on each set of beliefs (Trading, Money, and Self). I recommend doing it in that order. Write the belief you're working on up at the top of the page.

Once you have done that, write as many beliefs as you can think of regarding it. Some beliefs may be quite large, others might be quite small. Some may be vague. Others may be highly specific.

For example, let's say we wrote, "Trading Beliefs" up at the top of our page. An example of a large trading belief is that "the market is an infinite stream of opportunity." An example of a smaller highly specific trading belief might be "the 21-day exponential moving average generally works well as a place for me to place my stop loss when other layers of confluence are in place."

WRITE YOUR BELIEFS

We literally have hundreds of beliefs linked to trading, money, and self. Do your best to write as many as you can. I've done this exercise dozens of times, and if this is your first time doing it, I know how daunting it can seem. However, the more you write, the more your mental garden will be weeded, so really push yourself here. The process can feel exhausting at times. If you feel you need a short break, take it. But come right back to it.

Awareness Exercise 2

Now that you've written out your beliefs, your next step is to figure out how you got them. Be warned. It's easy to fall into the trap of believing that we created these beliefs or that we gave them to ourselves. While our collection of beliefs and how they are linked together within our minds may be unique, each individual belief comes from the outside.

Let's go back to our computer example for a moment. When it was created, it started with some metals and plastic. Those were formed into circuit boards, casings, wires, and buttons. Later on, an operating system was installed, and then software was added. When we were born, we were born with a clean slate and the ability to take things in from our environment. As we grew and took more and more in from our environment, our freedom of choice developed. Our preferences developed. And we began making associations and various links in our minds.

For this exercise, we want to examine what our beliefs are linked to and where they originated from. This makes it a lot easier to discern a weed from a plant and how to untangle them.

With this in mind, think about the beliefs you wrote down. Were they given by a parent, relative, or guardian? Were they given by a teacher, mentor, or guide? Did they come from a book? Someone you admire or hold in high regard? Did they come from society, a religious institution, a school, work, or the government? Did these beliefs come from the news or from social media? A friend or someone passing us by in a restaurant, your local gym, or some other public place?

Next to each belief, write its point of origin.

You can do this on a sheet of paper following the setup below, or you can download our template at tradingmindwheel.com/resources.

BELIEF	POINT OF ORIGIN	LINKS

Awareness Exercise 3

Now that we have written out our beliefs and we know where they came from, we can begin to "deconstruct the code."

Ask yourself, in what ways are these beliefs attempting to serve you presently? Remember from the beginning of this chapter when we mentioned that *ALL BELIEFS ARE SERVING US*? Well, a belief can be like a line of code. It may have served us when it was first written. In what way(s) is it serving us now? Maybe this belief has become foundational. Maybe it's like a plant that has borne many fruits! Or instead, maybe this belief is one that we adopted as a bandage to help us through a tough period in our lives. Maybe it served its purpose and like all bandages, needs to be removed.

Becoming intimate with our beliefs in this way can help strengthen those beliefs that continue to serve us. It enables us to find new purposes and links for other beliefs that are useful but need some redirection or a fresh perspective. We can gently let go of those beliefs that served us in the past, fulfilled their purpose, and can now be put to rest.

Take your time with this part of the exercise. As you work your way through each of the beliefs you wrote down, ask, "In what ways is this belief serving me now?" and then ask, "In what ways did this belief serve me in the past?"

You can do this on a sheet of paper following the outline below (I find holding the page horizontally works best since the answers are getting longer), or you can download our template at tradingmindwheel.com/resources.

BELIEF	How it served in the past	How it is serving now

Awareness Exercise 4: Fear Not!

Many of us fear letting go of the past and for good reason. "Those who forget the past are doomed to repeat it" is a quote from George Santayana that echoed in my mind when I got to this part of the exercise. However, I later realized that "letting go of the past" and "forgetting the past" are two completely different things.

I'm reminded of one of the lessons Mark Douglas gave us in his book *Trading in The Zone* about beliefs. Once a belief is held, it's never "deleted" or as though it had never existed. It's still a part of our consciousness. However, the amount of energy we give our beliefs is what matters. The energy that a belief has is what strengthens or weakens it, gives it control or puts it in the back seat.

The energy that a belief has is in many ways similar to physical energy. Think of a time when you had incredible amounts of physical energy. When you felt as though you could do anything. Perhaps run through a brick wall. Maybe that time was earlier today. Maybe it was years ago. But you remember that energetic state, and you know what it's like to feel energized.

Now think of a time when you've felt low energy. Exhausted. Lethargic. Unable to move. We've all felt this at some point as well.

When it comes to beliefs, the more energy we give them, the stronger they are. The less energy we give them, the weaker they are. Reread those sentences because they're very important. *We have the ability to control the flow of energy.* The amount of energy a belief has is our choice!

For this exercise, our aim is to withdraw energy from the beliefs that are no longer serving us and *energize* the beliefs that *are* serving us. How do we do this? I've got some great news for you. In doing the prior exercises, we've already started the process.

To continue the process, a simple, lighthearted example that I like to use is a common childhood belief in Santa Claus (you could easily swap this with the Tooth Fairy, Easter Bunny, or if your name happens to be Linus and you're friends with Charlie Brown, the Great Pumpkin).

For most of us, a belief in Santa was a fairly strong one with lots of energy when we were children. Go to any mall in the '80s or '90s, and the line to sit on his lap, take a picture, and tell him what you wanted for Christmas often stretched for as far as the eye could see. Tell any of those kids that Santa wasn't real, and you'd likely get kicked in the shins!

As we grew up we eventually learned the truth and began to let go of the belief, at least in the way that it was initially held. Perhaps the belief morphed into one of kindness, giving, or generosity. In any case, the energy in the original belief was transformed, and in some ways lowered. We can still remember back to a time when the belief was strongly charged, but now the belief is no longer charged in the way it once was.

Exercise

Think back to a time when one of your childhood beliefs (Santa or something else if you didn't believe in Santa) began to change. Do you remember what brought on the change? Did you see something? Hear something? Did you ask questions? Or was it some combination thereof? We want to do something similar with the beliefs that are no longer serving us in a useful way. This will begin to lower the energy in those beliefs allowing us to reconcile them, change them into something more useful, and file them away.

For some beliefs that we've identified strongly with, held for a particularly long time, or are interwoven with some of our other beliefs, this de-energizing or "loosening" process (particularly the first time) can feel a little scary. It may even feel emotionally painful to some degree. Questioning our beliefs often can be. And to be honest, the first time I did this exercise I wept multiple times. I had to pause. Take breaks. And then persevere. Even now as I reflect back on this period in my life, a tear comes to my eyes. I can't promise you that this process will be painless. Growth is seldom painless.

However, I can promise you that it will be worth it. And the more we put into it, the more we will get out of it.

Four Stages of Letting Go

To begin, look at your answers in Awareness Exercise 3. For any of the beliefs that are no longer serving you, ask, "Can I let this belief go?" Answer in a binary way, simply yes or no, and try to move through the list relatively quickly.

After going through several of your beliefs you'll soon realize that there is a spectrum of sorts. Some beliefs you'll be able to easily let go of. Some will likely be a bit more complex. And there may be a few that you really struggle with. The best way I've found to do this exercise is to do it in stages.

Stage 1: Go through each belief and ask, "Can I let this belief go, yes or no?" The yeses are done, the nos we'll come back to.

Stage 2: Once you've separated the yeses and nos, go back to the nos and begin questioning them. Ask, "If this belief is not serving me, why am I having trouble letting it go?' See what comes back to you. Often the trouble lies in either the source of the belief, how the belief is interconnected to other beliefs, or a combination of the two. If the belief came from someone you respect, it may be difficult to let go. If the belief is connected to several other beliefs, it will need to be unraveled. This questioning and unraveling in itself may allow you to let go of some of those beliefs. If so, wonderful! Those are now done. For the others, move on to stage 3.

Stage 3: Look at the belief that isn't serving you and look at what it's linked to. Then question the link. Why is the link there? What would happen if these beliefs weren't linked? What would happen if they were separate? Just because they've been linked together for a period of time doesn't mean they must always be. Is it possible to unlink them? Is it possible for someone else to hold both of these beliefs separately or in a different way? If not, why? We live in a time where more and more of what humanity thought was impossible is being proven possible. Be persistent in your questioning.

As you do this exercise and begin withdrawing energy from those beliefs that are no longer serving you, remember that nothing is being deleted or forgotten. We can still access and revive these beliefs whenever we choose. We can use them in some other way that better serves us.

With the awareness that each of these exercises provides us, we have strengthened our freedom of choice. We are in control of our beliefs. Our beliefs are not in control of us.

To sum it up, when it comes to trading, there are three sets of beliefs we'll want to become intimately familiar with. These are:

1. Our beliefs about Trading;
2. Our beliefs about Money;
3. Our beliefs about Ourselves.

For each set of beliefs, do the following:

Step 1: Select which set of beliefs you'd like to work on (Trading, Money, Self) and write as many beliefs as you can think of regarding it.

Step 2: For each belief write where it originated from and what it is linked to.

Step 3: For each belief write in what way(s) it served you in the past and in what way(s) it is serving you presently.

Step 4: De-energize, redirect, or let go. Review what you've written. Smile. Place a check next to the beliefs that are serving you. Withdraw the energy from the beliefs that are no longer serving you. Redirect some of them in a manner that may serve you better presently. File the others away.

Repeat this exercise for each set of beliefs (Trading, Money, Self).

EMOTIONS AND EMOTIONALITY

The idea of beliefs having energy is very closely related to the ideas of emotions and emotionality.

Robin Sharma, best-selling author of *The Monk Who Sold His Ferrari* and *The 5 am Club* refers to the phenomena of emotions and emotionality in part as "Heart Set." Tony Robbins, world-renowned life coach, has said that "Emotion is Energy in Motion."

Thought of in this way, the beliefs we hold that have high levels of emotion attached to them have high levels of energy attached to them as well. The "heart set" and mindset are interconnected. When we feel that a certain belief is thought of, triggered, or challenged in some way and we feel a strong emotional pull, that's the heart set.

Here's another way to think about it. Emotion is to beliefs as Energy is to computer programs. If the program doesn't have a power source, it remains dormant. If the emotion attached to a belief is changed, redirected, or reduced, the belief itself may take on a different meaning.

Exploring beliefs and doing this inner work can help us heal emotional wounds. As those wounds are healed, we become more capable of achieving higher levels of success. This isn't to say that high levels of success are impossible to achieve without emotional healing. But given the option, isn't it better to run a race injury-free? How much further could we go? How much higher could we climb injury-free?

THE MARATHON

Sometimes healing a wound before we get started isn't an option. Other times we get started injury-free, and then life throws us a curveball that hurts us mid-race. It's at these points that we can either quit or persevere.

My first marathon was back in 2008 in NYC. The air was a crisp 38 degrees Fahrenheit that Sunday morning, and it was sunny. Waiting at the starting line standing around in shorts and a singlet for an hour was a bit on the cold side. Once we got going and by about mile three, running in shorts and a singlet felt great.

Things were going pretty well that day. I was pacing myself, taking in a unique view of the city I grew up in, and took the advice of one of my running mentors to simply enjoy this first race and high-five as many kids along the route as I could.

This race had special meaning for me, as I wasn't just running for myself, I was running with Fred's Team in support of pediatric cancer research at Memorial Sloan-Kettering Cancer Center.

At this point in my life, trading was still something I did on the side. My full-time job involved working with these children. It was a very special time in my life and one I'm quite grateful to have had. Working with children that have cancer taught me a certain kind of empathy that I'm not sure I'd have learned elsewhere.

You might think that it'd be a sad place to be every day, but it wasn't. We coordinated a lot of special events to help uplift everyone's spirits including proms, convocation, clowns, and much, much more. While working there, I hardly ever saw a sad face on anyone, including the parents. The place was genuinely upbeat with a strong sense of hope among the patients, the staff, and the parents.

So the race was going strong. As I approached mile 18 I saw some of the kids I was running for. The nurses brought several of them outside. They were standing there cheering, some of them attached to IV poles. I had just run 18 miles, but when I saw these kids, I felt like I had wings. I waved, cheered back for them, and high-fived each and every one of them.

As I left Manhattan and entered the Bronx, I was immediately greeted by a steep bridge. I got over it, and soon thereafter, life threw me one of those curveballs. I felt a blister rapidly developing on my right foot.

"Uh oh," I thought as I reached mile 20. "This sucks, is painful, and is slowing me down. Crap. What are my options?"

My mind started to race. As I mentioned, this was my first marathon. During our practice runs the furthest we ran was 20 miles. So with each step I took, it was the furthest I had run up to that point. And I had another 6.2 miles to go.

I was exhausted and in pain, and the thought of quitting briefly entered my mind as a tear came to my eye.

I thought back to some of the other runners I had seen along the way. One group was a team of blind runners. Yes, blind! They were linked together holding a rope while one sighted person led the way. Remarkable!

I thought back to the people who had come out to cheer me on. Melissa, my then girlfriend and now wife, was at mile 18 as well. I ran over to her, and she gave me the biggest hug and kiss despite the fact that I was a sweaty mess. "She must really love him," my future mother-in-law said.

Could I let them down? Could I let myself down? How about the children I was running for? Could I let them down too?

"NO!" I shouted at myself in the middle of the Bronx. Yes, I was in pain. Yes, I felt exhausted. But quitting was not an option I was going to take that day.

In our toughest moments, remembering our why is important. Remembering those around us, those who inspire us, those who support us, and those who we support is important. This can allow us to tap into additional energy when we need it the most. It can fire us up. David Goggins in his book *Can't Hurt Me* refers to this as "the cookie jar." A mental cookie jar filled with memories that help provide us with the fortitude to carry on. We are often much stronger than we think we are.

HEALING WOUNDS

Healing blisters in the middle of a marathon or healing emotional wounds in the middle of a trade may not be possible. While perseverance is helpful and necessary in the short term, actually dealing with the wounds as soon as possible thereafter is essential if we are to continue our progress.

As I crossed the finish line in Central Park I was elated. In fact, I was more than elated. I literally jumped across the finish line with both fists in the air shouting, "YES! YES!" I had done it, and I felt on top of the world! See the image of me completing the 2008 NYC Marathon on the next page.

I walked over to the person handing out the medals and received mine.
Then the throbbing began.
"Not good," I thought as I walked over to the photo area.

I took a photo, still smiling, still feeling triumphant. But soon after leaving the medal/photo area, the pain began to intensify.

I hobbled over to the medical tent, my foot feeling more and more like a soggy balloon. When I got there and started to unlace my shoe, my mind began racing again at the thought of what I might find. Blood? Puss? Would I still be able to hop on the subway and meet my friends and family downtown for pizza and beer?

Often when running long distances, runners will wear special socks and running shoes to help absorb some of the pounding their feet will inevitably take. We go in anticipating exhaustion and possible injury, but even with anticipating it, experiencing it for the first time was a bit frightening. Looking back, the feeling was quite similar to when I placed my first trade, the first series of trades, and each time I made an adjustment to my trading before I had a clue of what I was doing.

Thoughts such as "Am I executing these trades right?" "Have I thought through all the possible scenarios?" "What happens if I missed something?" "Will I reach my goals?" "Are my goals too lofty?" "Am I chasing a pipe dream?" "Am I wasting my time?" often flooded my mind. Have you felt this way? Have these or similar questions come to you? If so, you're far from alone. Most of the traders I've encountered through the years, from trading champions to professional money managers, to successful full-time and part-time traders, and novices and hobbyists alike, have asked themselves some form of these questions at some point in their journeys.

Not all wounds are clear and visible to us. Some of the wounds may not seem like wounds at all. They've been with us so long that they've become part of our identity.

What has been does not have to remain what is.

These wounds may be our "normal." However, what's come to feel normal to us, if left undealt with, at best becomes a ceiling on what we're able to achieve. At worst, refer back to the story of Jesse Livermore. How do I know this? Aside from personal study, years of research, and helping others with these traumas, I've experienced my own version of it firsthand.

WHEN WHITE KNUCKLING FAILS . . .

"White knuckling" is a term I picked up from my personal trainer, Tyron Grandison. One day early in my training with him, he observed me gripping the barbell extra tight as I struggled with a lift. "Stop! Put it down," he said. "You're *white-knuckling.* Loosen your grip a little as you lift that over your head. You'll be all right. I'm right here." He said this firmly. A former military man with great attention to detail.

"White knuckling" implies that not only is too much force being applied, but it's also being applied in the wrong areas and in an inefficient way.

At the gym, form matters, and movements are meant to be fluid. When they're not, something is off. Injuries can happen. And at the very least, it's a terribly inefficient use of energy.

When I started down the self-development and self-mastery road more than a decade ago, I found a plethora of motivational speakers. I listened to them, read their books, watched their videos, attended their events, and got amped up. I felt like I could run through walls and for quite some time thought that the way to keep this up was to persevere no matter what.

There's *some* truth here. However, I learned the hard way that I was missing a few key ingredients. The result: mental white knuckling. This white knuckling had a tendency to show up in the physical sense (my first marathon), in relationships through the years, and of course, in my trading.

I'd often refuse to let go of trades that were moving against me. This was less out of fear of loss or admitting a mistake (though I'd be lying if I said that it wasn't at least part of it) but more related to a warped sense of what perseverance and success meant. There was confusion around the various rules and signals I had adopted at the time as well.

This combination in my trading led to metaphysical poor form and white knuckling. I had thought perseverance meant hanging on the longest. Turns out, I was just white knuckling during that period. It took me years to realize that this mental white knuckling is an extremely poor substitute for form, fluidity, understanding, knowledge, and wisdom.

Here's another brief story to further illustrate the point.

I got heavy into meditation several years ago. As I went down that rabbit hole, I soon learned that there are many, *many* types of meditation, from simple breathing exercises to transcendental meditation where you repeat a mantra, to numerous forms of guided meditations. At first, I was a skeptic. I thought meditation was just about "letting your mind go blank" and would be a complete waste of time. I resisted. But as I went further down the self-development path, some form of daily meditation was a near-universal recommendation, so I decided to give it a shot.

I committed to two weeks of guided meditation practice through this app called Headspace. It started with brief three-minute breathing exercises. At the time, even that felt like an eternity. After a couple of days, I progressed to five minutes. Then 10 minutes. By the end of the first week, I was hooked, and I soon became a daily meditator.

Fast-forward about five or six months, and as I'm meditating I'm becoming more and more aware of my thinking. Thoughts appear in my mind, but I'm associating myself with those thoughts far less frequently. This is similar in a way to the earlier exercises where we physically wrote out our beliefs. Taking beliefs out of our heads by writing them and physically putting them into the real world is an extraordinary gift we can give to ourselves. I've come to do this daily through various journaling exercises (more on this later). Developing our ability to slow down and identify thoughts, feelings, and emotions as they arise in the mind can help us create the space necessary to become far more objective.

Anyhow, back to the story.

We're entering the Spring of 2018. At this point, trading has been exceptional. I've already spoken at conferences across the United States, was a finalist in Benzinga's Global Fintech Competition, and was coaching traders virtually across the globe. All of this while still working the day job I told you about earlier.

When we're in places that we know we're not supposed to be, a level of frustration grows. It's like if you planted an oak tree in a pot. As a seedling, this may be okay, but eventually, it will outgrow the pot. It either needs to be transferred or the pot will break.

I didn't realize it, but I had grown and was at my breaking point. This caused me to become increasingly more frustrated with both my day job and my overall station in life. "What the f**k am I doing here" is the question that repeated more and more frequently in my mind.

I had recently begun a meditation practice where I would do some deep breathing exercises and then allow my breath to return to normal while continuously monitoring my breathing. After several minutes of this, I'd ask myself various types of questions and watch the various thoughts that would bubble to the surface.

On this particular day and during this particular meditation, I decided to ask myself why I had become so fearful. Why despite the strong success I was having in both my trading and in my other businesses was I becoming increasingly fearful day by day? Why was I choosing to stay in the pot when I was perfectly capable of uprooting myself? I had a track record. My finances were in order. Was I going insane? What was wrong with me?

Unlike other meditation sessions where answers would slowly bubble to the surface, today the answer leaped like a dolphin jumping out of the water. The answer was this:

I saw my younger self. The homeless, confused, and scared child we spoke of earlier. He was there, and he was afraid. He was fearful of the uncertainty that lay ahead. The association of loss of job (or in this case quitting a job) equating to a loss of a steady paycheck and that ultimately leading to homelessness is what had me feeling stuck, fearful, and frustrated, all at the same time.

Fear came from the inner child not wanting to experience this again. Frustration came from the adult who saw himself progressing in business and trading but who up until that point had ignored the inner child, not even knowing he was there but who rather was telling "some voice in my head" to "sit down and shut the F up." Well, that tactic didn't work because the end result was ultimately a glass ceiling forming over my head and a suffocating feeling of being stuck.

Often we may tell ourselves to "persevere." Perseverance, a "never say die" attitude, and standing up in the face of adversity are all great attributes that are universal to success. These are worth developing. However, we must be careful that perseverance does not turn into mental white knuckling. This is the difference between making it to the top of the mountain versus clinging to the side, unable to ascend higher.

For too long, I was white knuckling my way through trading, through my businesses, and through my day job. I was tired, exhausted, and oblivious. Well, perhaps not oblivious because that would imply a lack of awareness. I had often told that fear to "sit down and shut up" while I pushed forward. While it got me some of the short-term results I was after, it was also holding me back from the longer-term freedom I sought.

As I later discovered that day, the inner child simply needed a hug. He needed comfort. He needed reassurance from an adult that things would be okay. An assurance that he didn't have prior.

When we stop and ask ourselves what beliefs are driving or are connected to the emotions we're feeling, it is then that we're able to reconcile and begin the healing process.

MEDITATION IS A MARVELOUS TOOL!

Meditation can be a fantastic, potentially life-changing tool. Below is a brief outline of the meditations already mentioned plus a few others worth exploring. Research them on your own. I promise it will be worth the effort.

- Box breathing
- Transcendental meditation
- Guided meditation (Headspace is my personal favorite)
- Tony Robbins's "Priming Exercise"
- Brendan Burchard's "Release Meditation Technique"

SEEK CLARITY

A closely related cousin to awareness is clarity. When we have clarity, our paths become easier. Think of it like this. On a foggy day, how far can you see? If you've never experienced dense fog, the answer can sometimes be only a few hundred feet. However, on a clear night, how far can you see? Literally light-years! We can see the moon, planets, and even distant stars all with the naked eye. This is what mental clarity can be like.

So how do we obtain the mental equivalent of a clear starry night in our minds? The answer may seem overly simplified. Part of it comes from the journey and the consistent daily actions we take. You'll be happy to know that if you've done the exercises up to this point, you've already taken several steps toward clarity! Each of the exercises, stories, and sections of this book have built on one another and have hopefully brought you much clarity thus far.

Our next step in gaining clarity is to ask better questions.

Yes, I realize "asking better questions" may seem a bit evasive and overly simplistic. It did to me too at first. But questions really are the answer! This is a lesson I've heard repeated by several brilliant minds including Jim Kwik, Brendon Burchard, Albert Einstein, and Jason "JRyze" Fonceca.

So how do we ask better questions?

There are multiple ways for us to ask better questions. Here are two tactics I've found particularly useful.

The GPS Approach: Beginning with the Desired Outcome

When using GPS on our phones, what do we do? We enter our desired destination and the GPS figures out the way to get there, right? Want to drive to a friend's house? Enter the exact location, the GPS will easily guide us there. Obstacles in the way? Traffic? Accidents? No problem! We'll be routed and rerouted until we arrive.

However, if we were to put something a lot more general into the GPS such as "East," who knows where we would end up. If I did that, I may end up in the Atlantic Ocean!

Our brains work in a similar way. Give it a specific destination, objective, or goal, and it will work on figuring out the path to get there. Give it a general destination and it will struggle.

Don't believe me? Let's try this experiment.

Put your pencil in the "start here" box. Try to find a way out of the start here box and end in the "finish" box. Take as much time as you need.

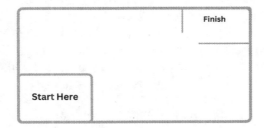

Were you able to figure out a way?

If you weren't able to figure out a way yet, don't feel bad. Most people don't on their first try. Let's get a bit more specific with our objective and see if it helps.

Put your pencil in the "start here" box. Find a way to the box with "finish" by any means necessary.

How fast were you able to get from "start here" to "finish"? How much easier was the task by adding only a bit more specificity?

Did you draw a straight line through the border around "start here"? Sometimes we may feel we need permission to draw outside the lines. Most of the time this isn't the case. When it comes to making money in the market, it's definitely not the case. If we develop the eight essential skills we're discussing in this book, you'll have the clarity to draw a straight line from where you're at to where you want to go.

Here's how this might play out with your trading.

Suppose your objective is to improve your trading performance over the next period. You've been actively journaling your trades and are in the process of doing a thorough post analysis (we'll cover strategies and tactics for effective journaling and post analysis in later chapters). In doing your post analysis, you discover that there are certain common factors among all your best trades over the prior period. Awesome! A question then comes to you.

"What would happen to my performance if I only placed trades that had these common characteristics?"

A very interesting question! However, it presupposes that we know where we want to go.

For some of us, that isn't a problem. We already have clarity on our goals, objectives, and values. We have an awareness of the results we'd like to achieve and the consequences we'd like to avoid.

But what if I don't know where I want to go?

This question of "not knowing where to go" is not all that uncommon. It may feel as though you're stuck to a certain degree. If you feel or have felt similarly, you're certainly not alone.

Some of the keys to getting unstuck include the beliefs exercises that we did earlier. Often what prevents us from moving forward are the "mental weeds" holding us back, particularly if we are unaware of them.

Often these kinds of "mental weeds" tie themselves to our need for certainty and, as such, are effective at holding us back.

For example, a childhood belief such as "If you're lost, you should stay put until someone finds you" is a fairly common example of a belief parents give their children. "Stay put until you're found" can help adults find lost children. However, while this may work and serve us well as a child, using this tactic as an adult can keep us stuck where we are. As adults, no one is coming to find us.

If we're uncertain of where to go, we need to start moving to figure it out. The only thing that is certain is that if we don't move, we'll stay exactly where we are. In life, we often get what we tolerate.

Are you happy with where you are? If you're not moving, or are continuing to move in the same direction you've been moving for a while, then you'll likely get more of the same. If we're not happy, we need to make a move.

We'll discuss planning moves and moving effectively in later chapters. Right now, let's discuss the thing keeping us in place. The "comfort zone."

The Comfort Zone

"But what if I move, and I make things worse?"

This is another question that comes up a lot. It is often linked to the comfort zone and traveling outside of it.

Below is a reproduction of the learning model of the various "zones" (comfort, fear, learning, and growth) and how we move through them.

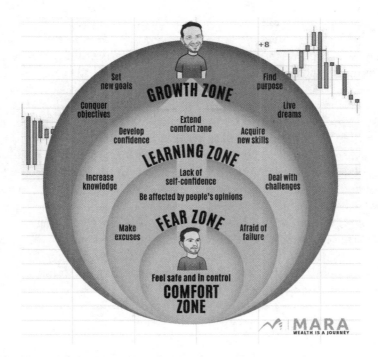

In this illustration, it's clear that in order for growth to happen, we must leave our comfort zones where we feel safe and in control. The more we leave our comfort zones, the more growth we can experience.

Is it possible to safely leave our comfort zones? If so, how?

Generally speaking, for most questions that begin with "Is it possible to . . ." the answer is yes. It's true here as well. Let's discuss the how.

The way for us to safely leave the comfort zone is to not go it alone. To get help. This can be in the form of books (like the one you're reading now), courses, mentorship, and coaching. Modeling success is one of the biggest shortcuts there is, and it comes in each of these forms. Getting around others who have successfully done what you're attempting to accomplish as well as other people who are also getting after it is the hack that finally led to my success in trading, as well as most other things. There's much truth in what Napoleon Hill said in *Think and Grow Rich*. We do tend to become the average of the five people we spend the most time with.

As the saying goes, "Iron sharpens iron." Get around others who have done what you're attempting to do as well as others who are striving toward similar goals. When I first started trading I was alone. I was able to leave my comfort zone, but I struggled mightily for nearly a decade. I kept bouncing between the learning and fear zones. Perseverance was, and still is, one of my core values. It kept me in the game and from retreating all the way back into my original comfort zone. But I made relatively little progress in my first 10 years.

In hindsight, it is no surprise that once I found a solid group that I could learn from, grow with, and contribute toward, I was able to turn the corner in my trading. And pretty rapidly at that.

I highly encourage you to get around others with a similar mindset and work ethic. I encourage you to go the extra mile and enlist the help of some coaches and get some mentors who have been in your shoes, who have already successfully made the journey and can help you.

Through the years I've been blessed to become fairly well connected. I have a large network of coaches and mentors I can connect you with that can help you attain the results you're after. If this sounds good to you and you'd like to learn more, go to tradingmindwheel.com/resources to get our list of recommended coaches and mentors.

Build Mental Funnels

There's a tactic for seeking clarity that I like to call the "mental funnel." Basically, we start with a broad idea and then progressively narrow our focus.

For example, suppose we want "a trading system that works." A worthy desire and, frankly, who doesn't want a system that works? Great.

Now let's consider the following:

- Works for whom?
- Executed by whom?
- What is required for the system to work?
- When are trades in this system executed? How often?
- What is the expected return of this system? What is the expected drawdown?

Those are just a few of the questions we might ask.

Any system we trade must be in alignment with our goals, beliefs, and ability to execute. Trouble is around the corner when any of those are missing.

Some of our desires may be quite large such as a five- or 10-year goal we've set for ourselves. Others may be small, such as an objective we hope to accomplish by the end of the week. In either case, "mental funnels" can help us narrow the playing field, focus, and optimize.

Brendon Burchard, a high-performance coach, says, "Clarity research tells us that successful people know the answers to certain fundamental questions: Who am I? (What do I value? What are my strengths and weaknesses?) What are my goals? What's my plan? Lack of clarity is strongly associated with neuroticism and negative emotions. This is why self-awareness is key to initial success."

Let's relate this back to trading. Again, the clearer we are, the higher we'll be able to perform. Break out the paper and pen. To get a free worksheet, go to tradingmindwheel.com/resources.

Who am I?

Let's get as specific as we can at this point.

Instead of writing something like "I am a trader," try adding more specificity to it by stating your ideal time frame and asset class. "I swing-trade stocks" is far more specific than "I am a trader."

Want to get more specific? Get into the qualities of the stocks you're trading. Do these stocks have any special characteristics? Do they only occur during certain periods or trend types?

An answer to this question may look like "I swing-trade growth stocks that are within stage 2 uptrends."

The remaining questions will help you gain even more clarity into the question "Who am I?"

What Do I Value?

List out the things you value as it pertains to trading. Values are a bit different from goals (we'll talk about goals in a minute). Values are more feeling based and are a bit more intangible. A few of the more common values relate to time, achievement, growth, love, self-direction, certainty, uncertainty, safety, and security. There's more, but I think you get the drift.

Some of the answers to what you value may have already come out in the beliefs exercises you did earlier. A few trading-related values you have may be related to overall return, reasons why trading interests you, what you consider to be acceptable drawdowns, the number of open positions you like to hold, the average number of trades you like to take within a year, and more.

What Are My Strengths and Weaknesses?

If we've done the exercises up to this point, we can begin chalking up self-awareness as a strength. What other strengths do you have as they pertain to trading? Depending on where you're at in your journey, you may be able to list many strengths and feel as though the metaphorical bicycle described in the introduction is pretty close to pristine. Maybe it could still use some polish or a new set of tires, but you're well on your way.

If you're earlier in your journey and have much to work on, the awareness you've built thus far is a strength. I encourage you to continue building this awareness. By becoming more familiar with the other essential skills needed for trading you'll be well ahead of the curve. Practice them well! Practice them with the intent to improve! As Mark Minervini discusses in his book *Mindset Secrets for Success*, practice perfectly. From there, you can begin developing those skills. Believe in yourself. I believe in you. You've got this!

What Are My Goals?

Perhaps the most effective goal-setting exercises come from another extraordinary high-performance coach, Jim Rohn. Here is a brief summary.

1. List as many of your goals as you can. Big goals, small goals, and everything in between. Things you'd like to accomplish. Things you'd like to have. Places you'd like to visit. Goals for your family (or perhaps your future family). New habits you'd like to have. Existing habits you'd like to break. Personal development goals. People you'd like to meet. Services you'd like to have. Properties you'd like to have. Ways you'd like to contribute to your community.

2. After you've written as many as you can (when I first did this exercise I came up with more than 100), next to each, write the number of years you think it will take to achieve it in the following increments. Which are 10-year goals, five-year goals, three-year goals, and one-year or less goals.

3. Take a look at all of your one-year or less goals, and circle the four most important.

4. Answer this: "To achieve these four goals I must become what?" (examples include: more disciplined, empathetic, organized, focused).

5. For each of the four goals you selected, write a few sentences or a paragraph about why each is so important. Why did it make the top four?

This exercise is so life-changing that I recommend you do it for both your life in general and for trading. You may only have a couple of dozen goals that are specifically related to trading, and that's okay. In doing both life goals and trading goals side by side, you'll begin to see how they are interconnected. For example, becoming a successful trader fulfilled a number of personal goals as well as much of what I value including time, self-direction, and financial freedom.

Here's a quick story to illustrate the point.

Last year my daughter started playing soccer. I had the freedom to attend *all* of her practices. Perhaps this may seem insignificant, but to me this was something very important. You see, when I went to live with my dad all those years ago, we were better off financially than had I stayed with my mom, but we weren't rich. My dad often had to work overtime in the evening and on weekends. While we were well provided for, unfortunately, this also meant that I didn't see him as much as I would have liked to. He wasn't able to attend most of my Little League games during elementary school or track meets and speech competitions in high school. At the time I didn't realize how much he was sacrificing for me. As painful as it is for me to write this, back then I had such low self-esteem and low self-worth that I thought he wasn't attending because I wasn't worth it.

Thankfully, where we start doesn't have to be where we stay. We can all course correct. I came to realize that the thoughts I had of "not being worth it" were untrue. I'm glad I figured that out in time. I'm extremely grateful to have been able to tell my dad how grateful I was for all that he did before he passed. While we are able to course correct, some opportunities don't last forever.

In the next section, we'll discuss the role S.M.A.R.T. goals play and how to set them. But first . . .

What's My Plan?

Answering these questions will help you develop your plan:

- How will we achieve all that we've laid out?
- Whose help should we seek?
- What should we learn more about?
- What actions must we take?
- How often must we take them?
- What are some of the obstacles that might get in our way?
- How will we deal with those obstacles when they occur?
- Can some of those obstacles be avoided? If so, how?

Our plans don't need to be elaborate. But they do need to be actionable, and they must be something we're able to execute well.

This book will help you develop better plans. Fully developed trading plans involve each of the eight essential trading skills and are often S.M.A.R.T.

S.M.A.R.T. Goals

S.M.A.R.T. It's more than just intelligence. It's an acronym that will help us create more actionable goals and achieve them.

We already know that a clear path is much easier to traverse than an unclear one. S.M.A.R.T. goals help take our clarity to the next level. Similar to pouring lighter fluid on a flame, if we really want to get going on our goals, make them S.M.A.R.T.

What Are S.M.A.R.T. Goals

S.M.A.R.T. goals are:

- Specific;
- Measurable;
- Achievable;
- Relevant; and
- Time-bound.

Let's take the goals from the earlier exercise that you marked as the four most important to you presently and make them S.M.A.R.T.

Here's a recent personal example to demonstrate.

One of my four most important goals this year was to stop overreaching, taking on more than I can reasonably handle. Overreaching is the type of problem that can end up stunting our progress. At best it leads to being good, not great at a number of things. At worst it can lead to a lot of stress and often many "half-dug holes." Ambitious people can fall into the overreaching trap quite easily if they're not careful. When things are going well, more opportunities will naturally come your way. It may feel difficult or perhaps even counterintuitive to limit yourself at this point and say no. In fact, having just learned about the comfort zone, we may think that taking on more than we can handle will help us stretch beyond our comfort zones and is a good thing. On the contrary, there's a fine line between pushing toward our outer limits and overreaching. A common trading example might be taking on more trades than you can reasonably handle, over-trading, if you will.

What we have tendencies for in one area of life can often show up in other areas of life as well. Cramming too much into a day? Attempting to lift too much, too fast at the gym? Sacrificing quality for quantity? The greater awareness we have in one area, the more light it can shine on others. If you find yourself spread out a bit too thin, a bit too often, perhaps you'll relate.

To be honest, I never thought I'd be writing a book, let alone two at this point. When my first book, *The MARA Mindshift Guide: A Trading Beliefs Workbook* debuted at #1 on Amazon's "Hot New Releases" and stayed there for six weeks, I was floored! When the opportunity arose to work with Wiley on this book, I leaped at it. At the time of the contract signing, I was still trading, coaching people one-on-one, developing what has become our MARA Elite Program, developing courses, building a name for myself on social media, building a podcast, and having several other smaller projects going on all at the same time. Things really seemed to be taking off . . . and I began overreaching.

One of the things I learned from Evan Carmichael is to assess opportunities based on whether or not it's a "hell yes." If it isn't, then it's a no. Do this regularly, and our lives inevitably become filled with many "hell yeses."

For me, writing this book and working with Wiley was a definite "hell yes." However, I had so many balls already up in the air that adding another eventually caused me to trip and fall flat on my face.

I thought I had a clear plan. I didn't. I leaped at an opportunity and tried to shoehorn it into everything else I had going on.

This overreach led to additional stress at home and working longer hours than I'd like. Don't get me wrong, I'm not complaining. I love what I do. I am extremely grateful and feel blessed to be in the position I am in. But I'm no guru. Even though I'm writing a book and practicing what I preach, I still slip up sometimes. Well, this slip-up led to some conflicts with other goals I had. Goals to be more present with my family. Goals to improve my mental and physical health. My daily energy started to diminish, which led to lower productivity and even more stress.

This can be a vicious cycle and is one of the reasons why clarity, planning, goal-setting, S.M.A.R.T. goals, and as we'll discuss later, journaling and post-analysis are so important. It helps us lay the most important elements out on the table, figure out a path, go, and course correct as necessary. It allows us to spiral up instead of spiraling out of control.

Having clarity on my goals and values helped me put my family first again. Reduced stress and greater joy at home gave me an energy boost. Improving my health by laying off sugar, increasing my water intake, giving up alcohol altogether (except for one drink on special occasions), and increasing my physical exercise (weight training, spin classes, and HIIT five days a week, and light stretching on weekends) plus a midday daily exercise consisting of a 20-minute walk around the neighborhood have led to both greater energy, greater focus, and far greater productivity.

Now that I was in a better mental state, I was able to better assess the various projects and develop solutions, some of which included making cuts, postponing others, getting help with a few, and focus.

One more thing about overreaching before we move on. What I've learned is that overreaching can sometimes be a form of greed. Wanting too much too fast, so that it ends up preventing us from getting what we want. The irony is that if we focus on just a few goals at a time (and why we narrowed it down to four) and add a little bit of patience, we can often achieve all that we want and a whole lot more, far faster than we ever dreamed possible.

Through this process of focused effort and all that we've discussed up to this point, I was able to hit 39 of my personal goals in just three months, four times faster than the year I thought it would take.

For a bit of contrast, here's how Mike from 20 years ago operated and got tripped up:

- Had a goal of wanting to make a bunch of money;
- Did not dig deeper into his why; had no idea what a S.M.A.R.T. goal was;
- Did *some* of what he considered research back then including watching MSNBC, Jim Cramer, and reading the occasional newspaper and magazine article.

That was it. I thought I was doing my homework and was well prepared, so I stopped there, thinking I was done. When things didn't go as planned, I proceeded to wonder why I kept getting caught in the "boom-bust" cycle, and whenever I'd make any money in the market, why I proceeded to give it all right back.

Here's how I made my goal to stop overreaching SMART and how you can apply this same methodology with any of the goals you have.

S (Specific): Stop overreaching by focusing on just one major project at a time until that project is complete.

M (Measurable): I measure this in blocks of time on my daily planner and write about it in my personal journal. I can see, both in real time as well as when I go back and review, how often I'm sticking with one major project at a time and how often I'm slipping up.

A (Achievable): At the time, "stopping overreaching" seemed near impossible. What about everything else I was doing? *"I don't want anything to* *slip through the cracks"* is what I often told myself, a simple yet powerful trick the mind uses to stay within the comfort zone. Growth requires change and often a bit of discomfort. I dropped the *"slip through the cracks"* story, made cuts and postponements, prioritized, and got help. Soon what I thought was nearly impossible became totally achievable.

R (Relevant): In reviewing all of the goals I had written for myself (including stopping overreaching) I quickly realized that stopping over-reaching was the most relevant, the most important, and a primary key for me to achieve every other goal I had on the list. I learned that some-times the things we need to stop doing are more important than the things we want to start. As the saying goes, "If we want to get ourselves out of a hole, first we must put down the shovel."

T (Time-bound): I wanted to start working to stop overreaching immedi-ately but knew that it takes time to install new habits. With focused effort and a solid plan, I was able to stop overreaching within about two months and have made a conscious effort to maintain this habit up to this day. It's not to say that I don't slip up occasionally, that I never feel a bit over-extended or overwhelmed. But given the other habits I've installed and skills I've developed (all discussed in this book), I check in regularly and am able to course correct whenever needed.

Are you beginning to see how one thing builds on the next? Are you starting to understand how mindset interconnects and is interwoven into everything? It's why we started here and why mindset is at the center of the trading mindwheel.

EQUANIMITY

Equanimity is a concept I learned from Ed Mylett, entrepreneur and best-selling author. I looked deeper into it, and in its broadest sense it refers to a state of calm. More specifically and how it can help us in trading is that it is the ability to let things go, both good and bad.

When we cling to things, that is when we open the door to feelings of loss or despair. Think about the person who has a great trade, is on high, wants more of that feeling, and clings to it. Rather than focusing on the next trade and opening the door for that feeling to reenter, clinging to the feeling of the prior trade shuts the door. Fear of coming off that high causes us to go backward. A lack of equanimity in this case gets us more of what we don't want.

The same thing happens on the other side of the coin as well. When you fear something bad, such as a losing streak, and are afraid it will never end, this sends you into despair. The problem in both cases is a lack of equanimity, a lack of not letting go.

As in the passage of time, trades will keep on moving, good ones, bad ones, ones that make us money and ones that cost us money (or as my friend Dr. Brett Steenbarger says, add to the positive learning PnL).

The more equanimity we have, the less emotional impact wins and losses have on us. We realize that both will come and both will go. Both are a natural part of trading.

Of course, our desire is to have a growing equity curve. The question then becomes how do we get it. The way we get it is by developing each of the eight essential trading skills discussed throughout this book.

This book provides you with the skeleton needed to stand. It shows you the meat and the customizations that I've developed for myself, the thought processes, and the rationale behind them, and how others have taken these and customized them for themselves and how you can, too.

JOURNALING: Step One of Accountability and Continuous Improvement

Understanding under what circumstances your trades work best and when they don't.

Perhaps the most underrated skill and the most underutilized tool in all of trading is that of journaling. . . . Yes, journaling!

Used well, it acts as a mirror showing us exactly where we're at, all the progress, all the flaws, all the details. By knowing where we're at, we can figure out what we need to do to get to where we want to go.

The same year that my trading finally turned the corner is the year I finally got serious about journaling my trades. There were a few other factors that came together as well, and I'd be remiss if I gave all the credit to journaling. Some of the other factors include consistent study and self-development, developing a routine that suited me and that I was able to execute well, and surrounding myself with other positive individuals who were pursuing similar goals. It was actually several members of the group I had joined that encouraged me to get serious about journaling my trades, so I did.

When I first started trading, I heard about journaling but thought it was a waste of time. A chore at best, and a chore that I didn't like doing. I didn't see the purpose or the upside at the time. Because I was closed-minded to journaling, when I attempted it, I struggled with it, was inconsistent with it, and my belief of it being a waste of time became a self-fulfilling prophecy.

Who needs to journal? I can remember my trades and why I bought and sold. Plus the broker has the log of all the orders, so I'm good to go!

That's what I thought at the time; closed-mindedness, dismissiveness, excuse-making.

As it turns out, success is the complete and polar opposite.

These attitudes kept me stuck for a long time. Until I became open-minded and willing to change, I couldn't move forward. It'd actually be impossible. *Remember what we discussed earlier in the book about our beliefs controlling our actions? If we continue believing the same things, we'll continue taking the same actions.*

So how did these beliefs finally change?

They changed with a little bit of grace, a touch of openness, and consistent action. This time grace came to me in the form of a gift. A co-worker gifted a copy of *How to Make Money in Stocks* by William O'Neil. Later on, grace came in the form of finding, attending, and being accepted into the

NYC Investor's Business Daily Meetup. Grace continued to come with openness, a desire to improve, and consistent action toward improvement.

I've learned that there are many forks along our paths. Where these forks lead is often shaped by our attitudes. Closed-mindedness, dismissiveness, and excuse-making all lead to dead ends.

WHAT TO JOURNAL ABOUT

Logging our trades and gathering data is important and a good first step. However, if we were to stop there, we would be leaving a lot on the table and we would be leaving out the most *interesting* parts!

Our aim is to journal with intent, meaning that our journaling has certain goals and purposes that we're after. There are three core elements to great journaling as well as a hierarchy to follow. I call it the **triad of great journaling.** This includes:

1. General Awareness;
2. Gathering Specific Data;
3. Focusing In on Our Objectives.

Taking action with the triad of great journaling not only propels us forward. It's like strapping a jet engine to the bicycle we discussed back in the introduction. Journaling is a skill that, as we develop it, helps us develop all of the other skills as well.

General Awareness

Our first goal with journaling is to create awareness. How could we possibly hope to improve, elevate, or evolve something that we are unaware of? A lawn may grow on its own by the graces of Mother Nature. However, a lush, vibrant lawn that you might find on a golf course takes a different skill set, and part of it includes awareness.

So what should we be aware of in our trading? For starters, **we must become aware of our patterns of thinking.**

Traders who find themselves stuck are often locked into a certain pattern of thinking. These patterns can include just about anything: (1) patterns of denial when trades sour; (2) patterns of giving trades more room than they deserve; (3) patterns of sizing too big or too small and at the wrong times; (4) patterns of unwaveringly following rules, a seemingly positive quality, but even when the results of following them have been subpar; *or* (5) patterns of feeling they've finally turned the corner and begin resting on all that got them there.

When we are unaware of these or other patterns of thinking, the patterns will often continue repeating. These patterns of thinking lead us to perform the same behaviors. And the same behaviors lead to the same results.

Unless we're thrilled with the results we're getting, our best first step toward getting better results is to generate awareness. And the irony—if you are thrilled with your results, you likely have a level of awareness about them.

We have the ability to become our own best advisors. In order to do this, we must become objective. By taking our thoughts out of our heads and placing them in a journal, we can review our thoughts objectively. This little bit of space we've created between us and our thinking by taking our thoughts out of our heads and placing them somewhere in the outside world is a large part of what allows us to be objective.

So what should we write in our trading journals to help create a general awareness?

For this part of our journal, we should write whatever thoughts come to mind. We may have thoughts about the market environment, a specific trade, or perhaps one or more of the other essential skills outlined in this book. We may write about something we feel particularly strongly about (positive or negative). We may write about something that is seemingly unrelated to trading or markets. Perhaps something about our day at work. Something that happened at home. Something that's affecting us in a meaningful way. Everything in life is interconnected. If something is on our minds, we should write about it. Writing creates awareness. Awareness enables us to discover the actions necessary to bring about the changes we want.

Gathering Specific Data

When it comes to trading, there is a *LOT* of data we can track. As we evolve throughout our trading journeys, the data we track will likely evolve too. This idea may feel overwhelming, and feeling overwhelmed may cause us to procrastinate.

Questions such as "How do I know what data I should track?" "How do I know what data will be useful?" "How do I know if the data I'm gathering is reliable?" tend to come up. These are all very good questions. There are a few schools of thought on each of them.

How Do We Know What Data We Should Track?

There's a basic set of data that I believe we should all track. Then there are finer details that may not be necessary for everyone. I've outlined exactly what I track and why below. All of the finer details I've marked with a "*" next to them. *Basics are italicized.*

Data I Track and Why

Data points	Why
Ticker	Identifies the trade I placed
Entry date	Identifies the date I took the trade
* Setup type	When trading multiple setup types, it's helpful to track the setup so we can monitor its performance.
* Stage count	This tells us how early or late a trade is in its move. (More on this in the chapters on Analysis.)
* Earnings date	When trading stocks, I find it important to know how close to or far I am from an earnings date.
* Gut feel	My initial gut reaction to the trade is important. This is different from emotion. I view gut feel as our experience talking to us. I track it on a 1–5 scale and can see how it evolves over time. It's rare that I take a trade under a 5, but tracking performance up and down the scale (trades that are scored 4 and 3, for example) has helped me adjust what I consider a 5 and thereby strengthen my gut.
Entry notes	Rationale and general analysis for the trade
* Sector	In real time, tracking sectors tells me if a group is heating up and if I'm too heavily weighted in a particular group.

* Trade grade	I grade each trade opportunity before taking it. In order to qualify for grading, a trade must: 1. Have a gut feel of 5; 2. Achieve a Trade Gauntlet Score of 5.5 or higher; 3. Be graded as A, B, or C.
* Trade gauntlet score	This is a score from a weighted average checklist I call the "Trade Gauntlet"™ of all of the key elements I want my trades to have. A perfect score is a 10, (More on this in the chapters on Analysis)
Annotated chart	When closing trades, include an annotated chart of where we entered, where we exited, and why.
Entry price	Price we entered at
Initial stop loss	Price I plan to exit at if I'm wrong; (more on stops in both the chapters on Risk Management and the chapters on Analysis)
Target price	Where we think the price can go
* Initial risk/ share in $	The difference between our entry price and initial stop loss in $
* Initial risk %	The difference between our entry price and initial stop loss in %. This amount actually becomes part of my selection criteria (more on this in the chapters on Analysis).
* Potential reward %	The reward % is based on the target. I'll typically only take trades where the reward % is at least 2x my initial risk, but often this is much higher.
* Reward-to-risk ratio	I always want this to be at least 2:1 and often much larger. The result doesn't always reach the target, but it's important for the potential to be there.
* Market Condition (at start of trade)	I break market conditions down into Red, Yellow, and Green. (More on this in the Analysis chapters.)

Average Closing Price	The tally of all our buys and sells for the trade. This gives us the average closing price.
Closing Date	The date we sold the last bit of our position
% Gain/Loss	What we made or lost in terms of %
* R Gain / Loss	What I made or lost in terms of multiples of my Risk (more on R multiples in the chapters on risk)
* Up days after breakout	How many days the trade has been up since breaking out
* Good closes after breakout	How many days the trade has closed high in its trading range after breaking out
* High watermark in $	The highest price achieved while I was in the trade
* Low watermark in $	The lowest price achieved while I was in the trade
* High watermark %	The highest % achieved from my buy point while I was in the trade
* High watermark R	The highest R multiple achieved from my buy point while I was in the trade
* Low watermark %	The lowest % achieved from my buy point while I was in the trade
* Low watermark R	The lowest R multiple achieved from my buy point while I was in the trade
Days held	How long I was in the trade
* # of danger signals day exited	There are a number of what I consider "danger signals," which when they begin to pile up tell me it's time to exit the trade.

* Asset class	If trading multiple assets, this is essential. If not, you can skip it. At the time of this writing, I trade stocks, options, and crypto.
Position size %	How much of our portfolio was allocated to this position in % terms. (More on this in the Risk Management chapters.)
Capital risked %	How much of our capital was risked on the trade. (More on this in the Risk Management chapters.)
* Trade type	If trading multiple styles, this is essential. If not, you can skip it. At the time of this writing, I predominantly swing-trade but find it helpful to break out the occasional long-term investment, short sale, and day trade.
Trade management plan notes	All notes that we've written about our trade throughout the life of the trade should be logged here. For example, I'll write notes on each of my trades every day, which include the overall feeling of the trade, chart, industry, and market-specific highlights, any present danger signals, any looming danger signals, and how I'll respond in accordance.
After-action report	When the trade is closed and we review the trade later on, here is where we'll write what went well with the trade, what can be improved, and any other key insights.

A common concern is that if we gather too much data, we may get bogged down in the data. If you've ever heard the term "analysis paralysis," part of it results from gathering too much data. However, the dilemma often lies in figuring out the difference between too much and not enough.

So what should we do?

What I've found to work best is to lean a little on the side of over-gathering rather than under-gathering, at least in the beginning. Yes, this can be a bit messy. However, much like a sculptor, it's better to have a little extra clay and remove what we find later to be unnecessary than to be halfway through our sculpture and realize we don't have enough.

Make sure that you are at least tracking the **basics, all of which are bolded.** From there, sprinkle in what you think will best serve you.

Focusing In on Our Objectives

As we progress in our trading journeys, our objectives evolve with us. As we evolve, so should our journaling.

Here's an example of an evolution that helped me realize that I was too often giving trades too much room to fluctuate and as a result leaving way too much money on the table.

For a couple of years, going back to 2011–2012, I was making steady progress in my trading and was finally seeing results. After years of under-performance, questioning whether or not trading was for me, and nearly giving up, not only did I beat the major indexes, I had about doubled their results. I was thrilled!

. . . And then it was post analysis time. We'll cover post analysis thoroughly in its own chapters, but for now I'll share with you that when I went back and looked at all of the trades I had logged, where I entered, where I exited, and my reasons why, I saw that I was too often giving trades way too much room. I was leaving a third, a half, or even more profit on the table! Back then my emotions went from feeling like a champ to feeling like a chump.

Was I being too hard on myself? Probably. But back then it did give me the motivation to look for solutions. One of the methods of finding solutions came by way of the data I was collecting in my journal.

To learn whether I was indeed giving back way too much in my trades or whether it was a type of hindsight bias I was experiencing, I began tracking the "high watermark" on each trade I took. The high watermark is the highest price the trade achieves while I'm still in it. I'd compare that level to my actual % gain/loss on the trade. By doing this, I was able to calculate on average how much I was leaving on the table and to develop rules to lock in more gains. We'll go through those rules in the Trade Management chapters of this book.

Again, depending on where you're at in your own trading journey, you may want to journal only the basics outlined in the table earlier, some or all of the advanced data points listed (marked with a "*"), or perhaps add a few of your own. Whatever you decide, realize that our journals are meant to evolve with us and are always meant to serve us.

TYPES OF JOURNALS

In trading there are several types of journals we can use. Each has its pluses and minuses. I've used each type and have outlined each type for you with the pluses and minuses I've found in each. The ones that have a "*" mark on are what I'm using now.

PHYSICAL JOURNALS

- **Marble or spiral bound notebook:** great for getting away from the screens, performing a "mind dump" of our thoughts, and staying organized. I used to print out my charts, annotate them, and paste them into these journals. As silly as it may sound, the primary downside to these types of journals for me is that they didn't feel special enough. They felt too much like grade school (which I wasn't a fan of).

- **Diary type w/ lined paper*:** all the benefits of the marble/spiral bound notebook but significantly higher quality. A hardcover, leather (or faux leather) cover, and ribbon bookmark help the journals feel more important and special to me. Maybe this is a bit loopy, but it helped me feel good about using it, and that little bit of extra positivity helped me develop the habit. That makes the journal worth its weight in gold to me.

- **Loose leaf binder:** these were convenient for a while. I'd print out charts, three-hole punch them, make notes on them, keep them in the binder, and use dividers in a variety of ways. The simplest (and what turned out to be the best) way for me to archive in this way was to keep the trades in chronological order and divide them into groups of winning trades and losing trades. As I flipped through the binder I was able to more easily spot patterns in this way. If I didn't move part of my journaling to electronic, I'd likely have kept up with the binders.

SPREADSHEETS*

- I used Excel for many years, and over the past few years switched exclusively to Google Sheets. Not only have I found it more easily accessible across devices, but I've also found it easier to code formulas, pull price/volume data, and share it with others. I keep all of the data mentioned earlier in this Google Sheet and am able to query the sheet, run pivot tables, and gain deep insights from the data. For example, I'm quickly able to assess my average gain/loss each month. My objective is to maintain at least a 2:1 gain versus loss each month. When this ratio begins to fall, I know quickly that I must make adjustments.

TRADING JOURNAL SOFTWARE

- These were great for the time I used them. Many of them were able to import trade data, tag trades, and do much of the manual labor I was doing in my spreadsheets automatically. However, as I evolved, I noticed that the conveniences that the journaling software provided were now becoming a ceiling. The problem with journaling software is that it's often not flexible enough. Want to begin tracking a new data point? Not all software allows you to do so. Meanwhile, in a Google Sheet, it is as simple as adding a fresh column.

Summary

Keeping a journal where we log our thoughts for general awareness, log our trades and trading data, and intentionally evolve the journals as we evolve ourselves is one of the most powerful tools in our arsenal. Journaling can act as a mirror reflecting our biases: how trading can/should adapt to fit our lifestyles, consistency, inconsistency, and doubts; where our focus is (e.g. outcomes vs process); market psychology (analysis/layers of confluence); risk and sizing; trade management; portfolio management; and post analysis schedule, stats, and tests.

As with pretty much everything we're going to cover, one of the big keys to success is going to be consistency. We want to consistently journal. We want to consistently review our journals.

I suggest journaling daily. Even if you don't have any open trades, you can write about your thoughts, feelings, and emotions. Even if you only write a sentence or two, the idea is to get into the habit of journaling daily. From there you can build and develop your journal in the ways that serve you best.

TRADING ROUTINES

There's a saying in the Marines: "We don't rise to the occasion. We fall to the level of our training."

What applies to the Marines applies just as well for us here in trading. We've already discussed a few sources of our training, including books, courses, coaches, and mentorship. How we structure all of that comes in the form of the routines we create for ourselves.

We all have routines whether we're conscious of it or not. A key to any great routine, trading or otherwise, is that it serves us and that it is consistent. For a long time, I had an unconscious routine of checking my trading account in the middle of the day whenever I'd get bored. It wasn't serving me, and it would often trigger me emotionally either to become overconfident or to fear losing.

We want to develop our routines consciously and ensure that they serve us. The most successful traders I've worked with through the years have all had routines that served them and that they followed consistently: routines for how they'd analyze markets and trades, routines for how they'd make trading decisions, routines for journaling and post analysis, and routines outside of trading for their health and wellness.

Routines help us achieve a level of automaticity. Even if there are certain tasks that we're doing manually, routines make it easier to perform those tasks. This is what allowed me to trade efficiently while working full time, blogging, and building my first set of trading businesses.

The Comfort Zone Trap

Once we've established a routine that fits us and is aligned with our goals, it's easy to become complacent with it. We've found our groove. We're comfortable. We can move on to the next thing. . . . This is true at first and can remain that way for a while. However, if we're not careful, we can fall into the trap of marrying our routines, and routines are not meant to be married. They're meant to serve us, not the other way around. Once we notice that they are no longer serving us, it's time for review and time for some changes.

Let's not confuse change with upheaval. Change can be large or small. It can be a relatively minor tweak. When caught early enough, many of the changes we make will be relatively minor. Catch a leak in your ceiling, and you may just need to replace a shingle or two on your roof. Let it go for too long, and you may end up needing an entirely new roof.

The trading equivalent of needing a new roof, a new ceiling, and nearly a new house happened to me soon after my daughter Lily was born.

Trading was going great, and my trading routine was serving me well. I had just come off consecutive years of doubling and tripling the return of the S&P 500. My blog and trading businesses were growing. I was even progressing in my day job (which at the time I saw as a career that I wanted to stick with and had no intention of leaving).

At that point my trading routine consisted of the following:

Weekend Routine:
- Screen for stocks passing my fundamental criteria*;
- Develop lists:
  - Universe List (stocks that passed my fundamental criteria);
  - A Focus List (stocks from the Universe List that were setting up);
  - An Action List (stocks from the Focus List that I planned on buying)*.
- Analyze the general market's health*;
- Place orders for stocks on the Action List using buy stop limit orders*.

Daily Routine:
- Check open positions near the close for any sell signals (execute if I saw sell signals);
- Recheck the Focus List to see whether I wanted to move anything onto the Action List;
- Analyze the general market's health;
- Place orders for stocks on the Action List using buy stop limit orders*;
- Adjust sell stops on Open Positions as needed.

Those marked with a "*" will be discussed in greater detail when we get to our section on Analysis.

Fairly straightforward, right? It was to me at the time. That's why I was dumbfounded when my performance started slipping after Lily was born, two to three months . . . maybe market conditions had changed (at least that's what I had told myself at the time). Six months later and I found myself back to being a boom/bust kind of trader. Not only that, I had put on some weight (if you consider an additional 50 lbs "some" weight).

I had gone from being a rapidly progressing trader, entrepreneur, coach, and middle manager in a renowned health care institution to feeling more like Joe Cross at the beginning of *Fat, Sick, and Nearly Dead*. A few years earlier I had completed my second marathon. Now I'd be lucky if I could run around the block without getting winded. The extra physical weight, poor diet, and trying to conduct the same routine as I had before becoming a dad led to a massive amount of stress. I developed an odd skin rash on my face and hands. And I sat there wondering what the heck happened.

Part of what happened was that I was doing (or attempting to do) the same pre-fatherhood routine now that I was post fatherhood without taking into account that there are a lot of new responsibilities with becoming a new dad.

Having had the early childhood that I had, I wanted to be present with Lily as often as possible. I felt at odds with myself when I had to work late either at the office, on my trading, or in my trading business. Not only that, my weekend trading routine, which normally would take 1–3 hours, now ballooned into 10+ hours. Diapers. Feeding. Crying. And then there was taking care of a newborn! (That's a joke.) But the truth is that just like how my pants no longer fit me, neither did my trading routine. My roof was about to cave in, and I needed to make immediate and massive changes. My health, marriage, trading, business, and career were all on the line. I needed to do a complete 180.

Remember earlier when we discussed grace and the idea of being open to grace? Well, it starts with awareness.

At the time, I didn't like what was happening but I was unaware that I was doing this to myself. I learned the hard way that this is what can happen when focus becomes tunnel vision. After going full-steam ahead with my nose to the grindstone for months, I had unwittingly been sacrificing my health, my family, and my friends. A long walk and a heartfelt chat with my wife, Melissa, provided me with the reality check I needed.

"Is this what you want?" Melissa asked me.

"What are you talking about?"

"You've done so much. You're doing so much. It's been exciting and wonderful. But what are you hoping to achieve at this point? You're working constantly. If it's not the day job, it's trading. If it's not trading, it's the trading business. You say you want this time with Lily. It's here in front of you. How long do you think this time with her will last?"

She was right, and I was gutted.

This was painful to hear but these were the questions that needed to be asked. Questions are the answer? They sure are! This doesn't make them any easier or pain-free.

What did I want?

I wanted it all! Is that too much to ask?

Fancy cars and houses? Sure those things are nice, but they've never been a huge deal to me. Stuff with little time to enjoy was not what I was after.

Freedom. That's what I was after. Freedom to do what I want, when I want, and how I wanted it. Freedom to serve. Freedom to make a difference. Freedom to grow and to achieve. It was working for quite a while, but when things change, so must we. Things had changed, but I hadn't. And now my roof was caving in.

A tough conversation was had. Now I was aware and ready for a little grace.

Soon after our conversation grace came. In this instance, it came in the form of a life coach (shout out to Beth Marconi), a new business partner (shout out to Adam Sarhan), and an incredibly understanding, forgiving, and supportive wife (thank you, Melissa).

A lot was happening all at once. As a first step to begin righting the ship, I had to hit the pause button.

But as soon as I began moving toward hitting the pause button, my thoughts began shifting from taking steps to get out of the mess I was in toward all the fallout hitting the pause button *would* have and why I should continue to *persevere.*

Sneaky how the mind can work, isn't it? Did you catch the subtlety in the wording? Remember, words matter! The words "would" and "persevere" jump out. "Would" is an assumption that presents a level of certainty about the future, and "perseverance" is a core value of mine.

Questions such as "What about all the progress I've made?" and "What about the subscribers I had that were relying on me?" started coming to mind.

As dire as my circumstances had become, they had become a part of my comfort zone. Messed up, right? I was rediscovering firsthand that our comfort zones aren't always that comfortable. They can be just what we're familiar with and used to. We might cling to them whether they're serving us or not. At this point, the thoughts in my head were giving me tons of reasons to stay in my comfort zone and hit the procrastinate button instead.

Remember our discussion on clarity and the exercise of drawing a line from one corner of the box to the other? When we're clear, it's far easier to get from point A to point B. I thought I was clear on what I wanted. I wasn't. The mess I was in was the result.

After speaking with, and game-planning with my new team, Beth, Adam, and Melissa, I was able to hit pause and begin laying the groundwork to move forward.

Beth and I created a health and wellness regimen that included getting physically fit again, eating well, drinking water (a lot of it), and reorganizing my schedule into manageable blocks of time. Without our physical health, nothing else works.

Adam and I restructured the business. He began running the day-to-day and providing research and analysis to clients. This took a load off me and allowed me to refocus. It gave me the time I wanted to dedicate to Lily and provided the space I needed to begin working on the business instead of in the business. I began to realize that my passion for teaching, coaching, and mentoring was rekindled and evolved.

Routine Installation

As noted earlier in the mindset chapters, the difference between success and failure often comes down to our habits and routines. Install great habits. Get great outcomes. The habits we have go hand in hand with the routines we follow.

So What Makes for a Successful Trading Routine?

At its core, it must be one that we're able to follow consistently. If we can't follow it consistently, what's the point? It will be of little use to us. It's better to be able to execute consistently once a week than haphazardly every couple of days or so. Even in that phrase "every couple of days or so" you can see the lack of commitment. Our routines, especially in the installation stage, need to be executed come hell or high water. That needs to be our attitude going in, or else it isn't a priority. If it isn't a priority, it's unlikely to stick.

For example, a trader I was working with had asked how often she should journal her trades. Given her trading style, lifestyle, and situation, I suggested that she journal daily following the triad of great journaling.

"But what if I don't place any trades?" she asked.

"Journal that you didn't place any trades," I replied.

"But what if something comes up like an emergency, and I don't have time to journal?"

First, an emergency that puts us in a position where we're unable to write a single sentence or even a word that says "emergency" in our journal is possible but is hopefully few and far between. The occasional emergency shouldn't be a deterrent to journaling. And if we are having those kinds of emergencies frequently, then we should prioritize finding a solution for those emergencies so that they're no longer interfering with the rest of our lives.

The word "emergency" is often a trigger for something that is valid, plausible, and important. However, it is often a sly term the mind uses to stay in its comfort zone. To remedy this, let's clearly define and think through what constitutes an emergency.

Take a moment, grab something to write with, and think through the types of things that may come up. Anything at all that may knock you off course. List out as many as you can. You're likely able to list out many things that may come up, but how many are *true* emergencies?

Here's another question to ask ourselves, How important is installing this new habit? If it truly is important, how will you respond in those different situations you listed? What can be shifted in your schedule to make sure the journaling gets done? Even if the journal entry is just one sentence before you pass out from exhaustion at the end of a rough day, it's better than blowing it off! The reason is that you're sending a signal to your brain of how important this new habit is, that you're dedicated to it, and in doing so, you're developing your will to win.

For now, take out your log, (if you have a journal, put your routine front and center). And we'll make the following categories:

- Analysis: Trade Analysis / Market Analysis;
- Management: Trade Management / Portfolio Management;
- Journaling;
- Post Analysis;
- Testing, Education, Self-Development;
- Health and Wellness;
- Rest.

I include health and wellness and rest as part of the trading routine because both impact our overall performance. I've found that the more I've improved my overall health and well-being, the better I've performed in trading, business, and all other aspects of my life.

So what do I do personally? Below is an outline of my daily routine. I'm sharing this with you as one example to help express the level of detail involved. While some of the details may not necessarily be a great fit for you, using this as a template in designing your own daily routine and making sure that you hit on each of the categories will be helpful.

Wake 4:30 a.m.	I wasn't always a morning person. When I learned the benefits of waking early, I gave it a shot, struggled for a while, and it got easier.
Wash and dress 4:40 a.m.	Washing and dressing immediately helps me wake up.
Drink 10 oz. of water w/Athletic Greens 4:45 a.m.	Starts the hydration process and makes sure I intake the vitamins and minerals my body needs
4:50 a.m. 1–2 minutes of breathing exercises	Helps calm and focus my mind
5:00 a.m. Exercise	Monday–Friday I'm at the gym doing weight lifting, HIIT, or Spin Classes. On Saturday and Sunday, I'll do light Yoga.
6–6:30 a.m.-ish Relax/meditate	Here I'll open up the Headspace app and use that for 10–20 minutes.
7:00 a.m. Shower	I'll vary the temperature. Hot and cold. A cold shower can often be invigorating. I'll do this depending on my mood.
7:30 a.m. Breakfast/ family time	Breakfast tends to be light to moderate. Parfaits some days. Omelets others. I generally try to get in some protein, some fruit, and some vegetables.
9:00 a.m. Trading day begins	The prep was all done the evening before. I've already thought through the best- and worst-case scenarios and planned for both. This is a time of reflection, re-familiarizing myself with the plan, and reciting affirmations. I'll then check in with our groups and aim to bring value and positivity to them.

9:30 am–1 p.m. Projects and coaching calls	I've tracked my energy levels and my productivity levels for various kinds of work (creative, administrative, analysis, and learning) and have found that I do my best creative work earlier in the day.
1–2 p.m. Lunch/2nd wind workout	Lunch is generally light to moderate depending on how the day is flowing. More protein, vegetables, and fruit. The 2nd wind workout (thank you, Robin Sharma) is a light midday workout to revitalize me. (I feel great after the morning workout. Why do it only once a day?) Generally, this consists of a 20–30-minute walk or bike ride around my neighborhood while listening to an audiobook.
2–3 p.m. Projects, coaching calls, public-facing time, emails	This tends to be a catch-all time block. While writing this book, I basically cleared my calendar, and "project time" was just the book. Pre/Post-publication can be interview time, live streams, replying to messages on social media, and answering emails.
3–4 p.m. Manage open positions (see I do trade)	I've developed my system in such a way that the close is the most important time for me to be engaged in the market. Even here, I'm simply reviewing signals and plans and getting ready to execute.
4–6 p.m. Market/trade analysis, education	Here is where I'll update my "Market Mood" log (more on this in the Analysis section). Analyze open positions and make any adjustments to them. Run screens over my Universe List and see both the quantity and quality of setups. If I find anything I like, I'll place orders for them for the following day. All of this goes into my trading journal. I'll also typically fit in 30–60 minutes of education. This can be reading, taking a course, or listening to an audiobook.

6–9 p.m. Dinner / family time	More protein and vegetables at dinner time. I've cut dessert and alcohol for the most part although if it's a special occasion I'll splurge. I've also journaled sugar/alcohol intake before and after for several months and saw clear and noticeable differences in my levels of energy the following day.
9–9:30 p.m. Screens off, wind down, read, journal, get ready for bed	Rest and recovery are critical, and much of it happens when we're sleeping. Consistent sleep and wake-up times have helped me go to sleep faster and sleep deeper. Studies have shown that the reason for this is that a regular sleep cycle helps the body produce melatonin, the hormone that helps the body sleep.
9:30 p.m. (the latest)	In bed and going to sleep

This is the routine I have at the time of this writing, and presently it is serving me well. It is fully balanced for me. I'm the healthiest I've ever been. I feel vibrant and energized. I'm doing work that I love. I'm serving others and trading extremely well. I am continuing to grow. And I have more time for my family than I've had at just about any other point in my adult life.

While this may all sound wonderful, I'm far from perfect and am in no way married to this routine. I'll deviate from time to time. Special events, speaking gigs, holidays, and family vacations call for some temporary changes to the routine. It's easy for me to have these short breaks from the routine and then get right back into the swing of things because I've already successfully installed them. I have achieved momentum with them.

Make no mistake though. The moment this routine stops serving me is the moment I'll change it up.

SPOKE 2

ANALYSIS: Analyzing Trades and Markets

In this chapter we're going to get into the nuts and bolts of analysis, including the various types of analysis, what they're useful for, a framework for how to construct your analysis, and a whole lot more.

Like many, when I first got serious about trading, I thought that analysis *was* trading. I thought the better my analysis was, the better my results would be. I dove into the world of fundamental analysis and technical analysis, and I even started studying psychological analysis as it pertained to markets. My idea at the time was that if I were armed with superior analysis, success and riches would be around the corner.

It turns out I wasn't alone in this line of thinking. Log onto Twitter, Instagram, YouTube, StockTwits, or even a quick Google search on "stock market" or "trading stocks," and you'll be hit in the face with loads of information mostly related to research and analysis.

There's some truth in the idea that better analysis will yield better results. Analysis is one of the essential skills of trading and a spoke on the mindwheel after all. However, it's just *one* of the skills. Stop here like most do and how I did for a long time, and you'll learn the hard way that even if we become great at analysis, a bicycle with a partially inflated tire still doesn't ride very well.

THREE THINGS I LEARNED THE HARD WAY ABOUT TRADING

Hopefully seeing these mistakes, incorrect patterns of thinking, and where they can lead will help you to avoid making the same types of errors that I did.

1. As Green as Can Be

It was a warm summer's day near the end of June 1999. I was working part time as a messenger at my local hospital. I'd answer a pager (remember those?) and deliver various things throughout the hospital. It was my first job that paid above minimum wage out of high school. After about a year of working there, I had managed to save up $5,000, which was a lot of money to me at the time. I had enough for what I thought would be my initial stake in the market.

In case you didn't know, 1999 is the period commonly referred to as the dot-com bubble. The chart of the NASDAQ (see Fig 2.1) shows how prices were moving back then and where I had entered.

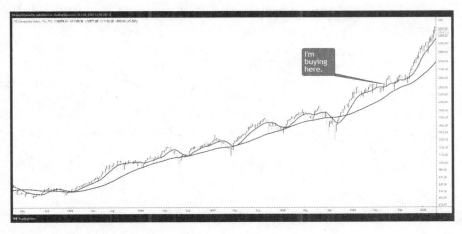

FIG 2.1

Not a bad time at all to enter and get started, right? Anyhow, back to our story.

I was a young and naive 18-year-old who didn't even know what a broker was yet, let alone anything about how markets worked. So where did I go to invest in stocks? I went down to my local bank! They happened to have a financial booth, which caught my attention, so I went over there.

As I sat in the waiting area, anticipation flooded my mind. All the wealth I was about to build. My financial dreams were about to come true. I'd put this $5,000 into the market, wait a couple of years, and a lot more money would appear in my account. Pretty easy, right?

Yes, back then this is how I thought the market worked. Back then, I thought of investing in the same way as I thought about planting trees. We dig a hole, put a seed in the ground, and Mother Nature would take care of the rest. As it turned out, I didn't know much about agriculture back then either. I learned the hard way that just like planting a tree, the where, when, and how matters a lot to whether our account thrives or dies. I had absolutely no idea what I was getting myself into.

After a few minutes, a tall, relatively young guy, only a few years older than me, wearing a suit came over to me and asked, "How can I help you, friend?"

"I'd like to buy some stocks," I said.

"Whoa, you don't want to do that!" he said. "Way too risky. What you want is this." He then handed me a pile of the prospectuses to the mutual funds the bank had to offer.

"We can do your investing for you and give you a lot more diversification than you can get on your own. Being diversified is one of the only ways to stay safe when investing. These prospectuses tell you all about the different funds, how aggressive or conservative they are, and what they actually buy and sell."

"Wow, this sounds great. Thank you!" I told him.

Looking back, he was right that I hadn't the slightest idea what I was doing. I knew nothing about the market, stocks, or even how or where to invest. Putting all of my money into something when I was this clueless would have been the financial equivalent of taking all of my money to the roulette wheel!

The bank's guidance was better than having no guidance at all. However, as I would later learn, handing money over to "the pros" is not a great remedy for ignorance, nor does it really take much of the risk away at all.

I sat with the prospectuses and began reading them page by page. After about 10 minutes or so another man, by the looks of him I'd guess he was in his 50s and who I assumed was the manager, came over to me. He looked over my shoulder and asked, "What are you reading there, son?"

"Oh, I'm reading these prospectuses. The other gentleman handed them to me and—"

"No one reads those!" He said with a laugh.

"Oh, okay," I replied, feeling foolish. I flipped through them a bit faster and finally said, "I'll take these two, and this one." I had chosen two stock mutual funds and a bond fund.

As I left the bank I felt smart and like I was beginning to take charge of my personal finances. I was doing everything by the book, or so I thought. I hired the pros to manage my money for me. I had loads of diversification (at least that's what they told me) with all those mutual funds. Plus I had time on my side! I wasn't planning on taking the money out until I graduated college in another three years. This was brilliant!

Three months had passed. I logged into my account to check my balance. To my amazement, it had already grown by 10%!

"Holy s**t I'm gonna be rich!" I thought to myself. I could already smell the upholstery in the new Jeep (I was into Jeeps back then) I was going to buy as a graduation gift to myself. I imagined myself driving down the beach with the wind blowing, the doors and top removed, and my friends in the seats beside me. It was going to be great!

Seeing the growth in my account had me feeling confident and a bit cocky. My plan was already coming together nicely. Even better than expected.

As time went on I didn't look at my account again. To be honest, my studies were getting more and more challenging, and I had forgotten about the account. That's okay though the *pros* were managing it for me, and they were already doing a fantastic job. I had results and I had real data—three solid months of it! I extrapolated it all and projected that I'd have about $15,000 in my account after another three years. What could possibly go wrong?

Fast-forward to June 2002. I had finally completed my senior projects and it was time for me to graduate. I then remembered my mutual funds, the wonderful responsible professionals at the bank that were managing it for me, and the beach I'd soon be driving down in my brand-new Jeep.

FIG 2.2

The mood quickly changed, however, when I logged back into my account. It hadn't tripled as I had forecasted. It hadn't doubled. It hadn't even grown by 50% in three years. No, instead after three years I found that my account was down 20% from my initial investment. I only had $4,000 left in it.

"What the f**k?!" I thought to myself. I did everything I was supposed to, didn't I? I had plenty of time on my side for my account to grow. I had the safety of lots of diversification. I even had the pros handling my money for me. How in the world was I down after three whole years? I was pissed. All that time wasted! Less money than when I had started! Oh, and to top it off, I still had to pay management fees for the privilege! Yes, despite the fact that they'd lost money, I still had to pay their management fees.

"Man, I would've been better off keeping that money in my savings account to accrue 0.3% interest each year," I thought glumly to myself. Financially, I would have been better off, at least in the short run.

So what did I learn from this?

Perspective is a funny thing, and it often comes to us with time and reflection. Looking back, as painful as that experience was then, it's easy to see now that it was a relatively inexpensive lesson the market had given me, and I am quite grateful for it. We all must learn the lessons of the market. Whether these lessons come cheap or expensive is mostly up to us.

After this debacle, I took a break from the market, thinking it was rigged.

Would I have reacted that way had I won? Probably not, to be honest. I'd have been a lot happier at the time, but I'd have the money and not the lesson. Better to have a cheap lesson that helps us make a fortune in the long run than to have a cheap win that costs us a fortune in the long run.

As they say, time heals all wounds. Despite the pain from that initial loss, there was still a huge positive takeaway. I had experienced firsthand putting money into the market and seeing it grow rapidly. This wasn't just theory or hearsay anymore. Yes, I made more than a few mistakes, but the possibilities were real.

2. The Cautious Skeptic

Here's an important lesson that I wish I had learned earlier. I've decided to highlight it here to help make sure you don't make the same mistake.

Making broad generalizations, like lumping all "pros" together, is something that kept me stuck for many years. Remember how important words and definitions are? I wasn't very discerning back then, so my idea of a "pro" was anyone to whom I handed money for a service. Clearly, this definition went far beyond bankers and mutual fund managers. Any coach, mentor, or financial service provider fell into my definition of a "pro." Since this was the case, who was I going to learn from?

I've met many traders through the years who were stuck in similar ways. How often do we find ourselves making broad generalizations based on one or a handful of experiences? This is actually a natural human tendency. We developed this as a species thousands of years ago back in the caveman days. It was a survival technique. The reptilian part of our brains learned to make these broad generalizations, and it kept us safe. When we heard a rustling in the trees, we'd assume *danger* and hide. This kept us from being eaten! Even if at times that rustling was just a squirrel looking for a nut.

Clearly, evolving beyond this point will benefit our lives in a multitude of ways. For trading, it's essential. "Trust but verify!" is a great motto, one that Ronald Reagan is often credited for. However, it is actually part of a Russian proverb. Reagan knew that one of the methods to establish trust is to learn and understand the language of the people to whom you're speaking.

In what ways do you think we can begin to learn the language of the market?

Back to the Story

When I was finally ready to give the market another shot, I swore that I would learn from my mistakes. Still sore from having trusted the "pros," I decided I would never trust them again.

I was flipping through the channels (NBC, Fox, etc.) one day and found a guy giving out free advice. He was yelling into the camera. Hitting buttons to buy and sell. He was very different from the pros I had met at the bank. Some of his antics were a bit silly, I must admit, but he seemed to know what he was doing. I found myself both entertained and actually feeling like I was learning something. The guy I had found was Jim Cramer.

As I'd figure out later, to a blank or near blank slate, just about anything can appear educational. At the time, I didn't know what I didn't know. So I watched Jim's *Mad Money* show and read some of his books. I assumed I was being taught all that I needed to know about the market.

Learning *all* that I needed to know about the market from a 60-minute TV show and a couple of books? How ridiculous, right? Rereading that sentence to myself has me cracking up! Yes, I was going to learn all that I needed to know about the market from watching a TV show and reading two or three books. Maybe next I would flip the channel and start watching the TV show *Scrubs* and in another week or two I'd be performing surgery!

A Little Wiser—but a Long Way to Go!

I learned the hard way that a good company in a hot sector does not necessarily make a good stock and vice versa.

One of the methods I picked up from Jim, and in fairness perhaps misunderstood at the time, was that if you like the story of a company and you buy the stock, stick with that stock until the story changes. If the stock goes down and the story hasn't changed, it's an opportunity to buy more.

To the essentially blank slate that I was at the time, this logic sounded reasonable enough. Stocks don't go straight up. They sell off sometimes. If nothing has really changed with the company and the stock is down, why not buy more at a discount?

Well, as it turns out there's at least one major thing I hadn't considered: How do we know when the story changes?

At the time, I remember reading about the airline industry getting ready to take off (no pun intended). Companies such as Delta, Jet Blue, and United Airlines were heading higher. So was Boeing. I learned about "cousin stock theory" from Jim and how if a certain industry is heating up, other related industries may be next. If airlines were heating up, how about the parts suppliers?

I did my research, which at the time included watching his show and reading what I found on Yahoo Finance, and found a company that manufactured and supplied latches to the overhead bins for commercial aircrafts. Perfect! With Delta, United Airlines, Jet Blue, and Boeing all taking off, I thought buying into this parts supplier made a whole lot of sense and went into it with about 20% of my account.

I remember buying in at around $14/share. A few weeks after buying, the price moved up to $14.50. Then $15. Then $15.54 (that price sticks out in my mind for some reason). Shortly after that, the price began to fall.

I checked the news and searched on Yahoo and Google. I couldn't find anything. Price was back to $14. A week later it was $13. Then $12. Still no news, and other stocks in the airline industry seemed to be doing fine. The story hadn't changed as far as I could tell.

"Hey," I thought, "maybe this is one of those times when the market is throwing me a discount and I should be buying more!"

I added another 20% of my account to this stock (which I still can't remember the name of and am starting to think my mind has purposefully blocked it out) bringing my total allocation to over 40%.

The problem with the philosophy of buying more at a discounted price is that each time the price moves against us, it becomes a reason to buy.

Rather than thinking of stocks like a piece of clothing or our favorite box of cereal, what if we thought about it like a $250,000 Lamborghini? If we saw that same one selling at $200,000 it'd be a steal, right? Maybe. But what happens when the price of that Lamborghini is cut in half and is selling at $125,000? Is it still a steal or is something wrong with the car and we are the ones about to get ripped off?

As it turns out, buying more as price moves against us is the exact opposite of what we should be doing. As we'll discuss more in the chapters under Spoke 4, "Trade Management," cutting losses short is the only way to prevent a small loss from turning into a big loss. I was about to learn this lesson the hard way.

When the price fell to $12 and I was down -14% rather than selling and taking a relatively small loss, I doubled my position. Having bought half at $14 and half at $12, now I only needed price to get to $13 and I'd already be back to even. "Genius!" I thought at the time.

Well, as you might have guessed, the price didn't go back to $13. It kept right on falling: $11, $10, $9.50. . . . Nearly a month had gone by, and there was still nothing in the news. Nothing on Google . . . "Maybe the dark web has something?" I questioned.

Jim was still taking live callers during his *Mad Money* show back then. I thought, if anyone could help me out, surely he could!

I called into the show early to secure my spot in line, about two hours before it was going to air. I remember closing the door to my office, blocking out my calendar, and patiently waiting on hold. The show started, and I was able to hear the show as I waited.

Eventually, the producer came on the line with me and said, "Okay, you're next. Are you ready? You're on!"

"This is Jim Cramer, welcome to *Mad Money*!"

"Booyah, Jim." One of his signature catchphrases that I parroted back to him.

"Booyah, Michael! What can I help you with today?"

"I have a question about (I gave him the ticker and name of the company). I bought this about two months ago, it went up for a little bit, but it's been falling for about a month and a half. What should I do?"

"Oh, the story on that one changed about a month and a half ago. I'd sell!" CLICK.

"Wait. What?!" I exclaimed, but the call had already ended.

I was left stupefied. How did he know that the story had changed? I had searched and searched and found nothing. Did Jim have inside information? Perhaps. Did I need to call into the show daily to find out if the story of a stock had changed? Maybe.

"F**k this!" I thought to myself. I sold the stock the next day, and it was back to the drawing board for me.

Ticked off, I had learned yet another very valuable lesson though I assure you, it didn't feel like it at the time. Here's the lesson: if we buy something and the price goes down from what we paid, that is all the proof we need that the timing of our initial buy was wrong.

Is it okay to be wrong? Absolutely. The question we must answer is, How wrong are we willing to be?

I didn't have an answer to that question, let alone a clear one. As it turns out whenever we don't have a clear answer for how wrong are we willing to be, the answer is "Whenever the loss becomes too painful to bear." The result is panic. We get desperate. Sometimes we may even call into a TV show. And we take a much bigger loss than what we had likely thought was even possible.

I was crushed. Not only did it feel devastating to have lost this badly again, but this time I had put in work. Lots of study. Lots of research. I did what I thought I was supposed to be doing. The market had dealt me an important life lesson. Unlike school, doing the work doesn't necessarily yield an "A" or, in this case, money in our accounts. No, sometimes we can do all the work and still lose. We can also learn the wrong things . . . or we can learn the right things, but in the wrong order and fail. Yes, the market was dishing out a full buffet of life lessons for me. Even though it was exactly what I needed, I wasn't ready to accept any of it just yet.

3. One More Try

I was now in my late 20s, a middle manager at a major hospital, and well into what I thought was going to be my lifelong career in health care administration. Was this the path I had dreamed about when I was a kid? No, far from it. But it was safe and secure and seemed to check all of the boxes of a "good job." I was bringing home a six-figure salary, had great health care benefits, and had about six weeks of vacation time plus holidays. Pretty good by most people's standards.

One day, John, my office mate at the time, approached me and offered this bit of advice. "Mike, you're a middle manager and making decent money. You should consider putting some of it into the stock market so it can start growing."

I nearly fell over in laughter.

"Ha! I've had more than a few experiences with the market, my friend!" I replied. "Let me tell you . . ."

I proceeded to tell him my tale of woe. How the bankers advised that I be widely diversified, let the pros manage my money, and sit and wait. How I'd watched and even called into TV shows, and how I bought on the way down. How I researched the company and despite that research, I still lost about 40% of my account.

John was a pretty nice guy, and he allowed me to rant and rave. When I was through, instead of pointing out the dozens of mistakes I had made and what I should have done, he simply said, "I know how hard it can be. I've been there as well. In fact, not many people here know this, but I worked on Wall Street for about 20 years before coming here."

"Twenty years? Wow! That's impressive. Why did you leave?"

"Stress," John replied. "The money was great, but working as a broker and seeing how people were treated was appalling."

He recounted a story where one of his friends was about to be fired. The night before this was to happen the manager had his friend's desk, chair, phone, and even his lamp put into the hallway along with the rest of his belongings. If that weren't enough to send a clear message, the manager also had a padlock installed on the door.

"Crazy, right?" John said. "From other people I knew in the industry, things weren't much better at other firms. So I decided to leave the financial industry altogether and came to work here. I still trade my own money and have done pretty well. I've used some of the profits I've made to buy rental properties in southern Florida. In the next few years, I plan on retiring. I'm going to sell my condo in Brooklyn and move to Nice (a city he frequented in southern France)."

"That sounds amazing," I replied.

"It takes a lot of time, effort, and experience to trade well, Mike. But trust me on this, it's worth the effort."

He leaned over. "Here are a couple of the books that got me started on the right track." John kept a massive pile of books in the office. They lined the shelves, were stacked behind him on a desk that wrapped around the wall, and he had even more under his desk, near his feet.

He pulled out a couple of books from under his desk. They were *Winning on Wall Street* by Martin Zweig and *How to Make Money in Stocks* by William O'Neil. "Read these," he said, "and let me know what you think."

"Awesome; thanks, John," I replied.

I took the books, but at this point, I was still living in my head and hanging onto the past, not quite convinced that I could ever do this. Sure, these books helped John, but if I read them and did the work, could I really expect the same results?

It was a long train ride home that night, but it gave me time to think. Eventually, I decided I had nothing really to lose, and so I started to read. Maybe the "third time's a charm" thing would work out for me.

So I started with Zweig and then read O'Neil. There were elements in Zweig that I really appreciated. For example, he outlined in great detail how he would use the newspaper to make trading decisions. What he would track and the specific changes he would look for. Awesome! I could see why John had recommended this one.

Then I read William O'Neil's book *How to Make Money in Stocks* and wow! If I told you that this book resonated, it'd be the understatement of the year. Everything in it made complete and total sense to me.

First, O'Neil discussed how he too struggled mightily at first and got kicked around by the market. His solution was to research all of the big winning stocks throughout history and analyze the characteristics they had when they were just starting to make their monster runs. He studied stocks like Bethlehem Steel, Walmart, Pick and Save, and thousands of others (more than 100 are displayed and annotated in his book). He studied the stocks making 200%, 300%, 500% some even 1000% or more in the span of only a year or so. He discussed the common fundamental characteristics these stocks had, the technical price patterns they displayed, and the market conditions in which they generally appear.

I didn't just read O'Neil's work. I devoured it. Digested it. And came back for seconds and thirds. I was feeling confident and felt as though I had a ton of clarity. The market was finally starting to make sense, if you know what I mean. However, unlike earlier, this time around I knew it would take significantly more than casually reading a book to produce results.

I reread the book a half dozen times. Marking it up. Taking notes. Attempting to annotate the charts in a similar way to how O'Neil had. Looking back, I was treating it like the courses I had taken in grad school.

And then it struck me—I needed to develop a curriculum for myself.

If I were to continue treating trading like a hobby, as I did in the past, I'd continue getting hobby-like results. If I started to take it seriously, maybe I'd have a shot.

Here's a lesson from Tony Robbins. "If we give a poor effort, what kind of results do you think we'll get? If you thought poor results, you're wrong" (that's what I thought at first too). "Poor effort doesn't yield any results. In fact, in the workplace, poor results will eventually get you fired." In the market, poor effort got me a −20% return after three years.

"If we give a good effort, what kind of results do we get? Poor results! That's right! And the unfortunate reality is good isn't good enough." A good effort in trading will *maybe* get us market results if we're lucky. But then what's the point? We could put our money into an indexed fund and save ourselves the trouble and much of the effort.

I know what you're thinking. You picked up this book and are like, "Hey, Mike, I'm not aiming for good, I'm aiming for *EXCELLENT*," right?

Heck yeah, you are! You're here to reach your maximum potential, but here's what I learned, and it's another unfortunate truth. Excellent effort only yields good results. But how is that fair? All this time, energy, and effort, and we only get *good* results? This is also something that I learned from Tony Robbins. Excellent effort once or a few times yields good results. Sustained excellent efforts compound. Sustained excellent efforts enabled me to retire from the corporate world before the age of 40. This is a level called *OUTSTANDING,* and all of the BIG REWARDS come when we move from excellent to outstanding! Outstanding is only fractionally more than excellent. For us in the Trading Mindwheel, it's mastering each of the eight essential skills, fully inflating the tires of our bike, upgrading it as we go, and continuing the ride.

Journeying from Excellent toward Outstanding

I learned that O'Neil had taken much of his early profits from the market and used them to fund his then-start-up Investor's Business Daily (IBD), a newspaper that would grow to rival the *Wall Street Journal.*

I read IBD every day and tried to follow along with their analysis. They would provide their own market calls and commentary and seemed to follow much of what O'Neil taught in *How to Make Money in Stocks.* "Perfect," I thought. "I'm finally getting a real education."

I progressed slowly. Slow progress is still progress, and I took it in stride. I wasn't blowing up my account as I had in the past. At the time, that was a major victory for me.

I remember coming across a small blurb in IBD that discussed local Meetups. People gathered together to discuss the paper, the CANSLIM methodology, and how they were applying it. "Great!" I thought. "This is precisely what I need!"

I showed up at my first Meetup. It was run by a couple of full-time traders and a private fund manager. There were experienced people in the audience and several newbies like me. The experience was wonderful! We met for three hours on a Wednesday evening, and I was completely blown away. The level of presentations at this event rivaled what I had just finished paying $60K for during grad school.

I soon made friends with the leaders of the group. Avi, Jim, Richard, and Curt. These were some really great people: open, kind, generous, and straightforward. The meetup would officially end at 9 p.m., and we'd often stay talking for another hour or so.

One of the major breakthroughs I had from them is that we can learn a strategy and then trade it in our own way. For example, we were all using O'Neil's strategy CANSLIM, but Avi leaned a little bit more on the fundamentals and the company's story. Richard and Jim leaned a bit more on the technicals and traded a little faster (holding for a few months if a trade worked out), and Curt provided me with my first glimpses into trading psychology and mindset.

I attended these meetups every month for a full year. Within that time I learned many of the fundamental skills that we'll soon discuss. Have I mentioned that there's no ceiling in trading or trading skill development? And that "outstanding" requires us to continue becoming the best version of ourselves?

In addition to developing my trading skills that year, I also had my first profitable year and actually beat the market. It was 2011, and I was up about 15% while the market (S&P 500) had returned about 13% that year.

Sure, a 2% beat may not sound all that impressive, but it was the first time I had done it. I didn't just "feel" like I was making progress. I finally had tangible results that backed it up.

I shared my results with the group and showed them how I had incorporated the many lessons they had taught me. I shared the trading journal spreadsheet I had developed and how I was tracking my personal stats, thoughts on trades, and market conditions. I shared the routine I had developed and how I had condensed it down, as we discussed in the earlier chapters.

They were so impressed with all I had done and in the way that I had done it that they invited me to become one of the group leaders and shared that they would like to adopt some of my processes.

"What?!" I exclaimed in disbelief. "You guys are the pros (the real pros). You guys are already successful. I'm learning from you. What could you possibly learn from me?"

"A lot," they said in unison. "The learning never stops."

I started to learn about this thing called the "beginner's mind." I had the beginner's mind, but so did they. Beginner's mind has less to do with our level of experience and more to do with an openness to learning. I've met many with little experience who lacked the beginner's mind and were therefore unable to begin. I've also met people with 30, 40, and even 50 years of experience who still maintained a beginner's mind. A beginner's mind is open to challenging currently held beliefs. Is continuously evolving. And is open to new perspectives.

Even though I was still a novice at this point, I had valuable insights to share. I had successfully taken what they had taught me and found ways to do it more efficiently. What was taking them several hours each day and a full day on weekends, I had condensed into 30–60 minutes a day total on weekdays and an hour or two on weekends.

Of course, it made sense why they wished to adopt some of my practices. Who wouldn't want a few more hours back in their day?

At this point, I was still struggling with some limiting beliefs related to personal self-worth, which is a big part of why I struggled to see the value they saw in me. These limiting beliefs were starting to be crowded out with a stronger set of beliefs and a far better environment, but they were still weighing on me.

"Dragons undealt with can never be defeated," as Robin Sharma said.

Well, there were still a few dragons that I had yet to deal with.

These issues manifested themselves both in my personal life and in my trading. My processes, analysis, and results were all improving. But even a perfectly designed trading system and plan can still be self-sabotaged.

I continued forward. The NYC IBD Meetup Leaders helped me, and as it turned out, I was helping them as well. I was honored and accepted the new role as an IBD Meetup Leader. It was a role that I held for nearly a decade.

ANALYZING TRADES AND ANALYZING MARKETS

I've come to realize two basic truths when it comes to analysis; we can analyze the thing (the trade), and we can analyze the environment the thing is in (the market). Both are important, and both can dramatically affect the interpretation of the other. Here's an example to help illustrate the point.

Imagine you're about to buy a brand-new Ferrari. You've made your appointment and walked into the dealership. The floors are shining. The salesperson greets you with a friendly smile. You're guided through the showroom and are enabled to select the perfect model and the perfect color. Sounds pretty good, right?

Now imagine the same Ferrari is for sale but instead of a gleaming showroom, it's being sold in the middle of a vacant lot. Aside from the overturned trash cans about 20 feet away, you notice a group of stray cats poking through the garbage. A salesperson wearing a plaid suit with elastic suspenders gives you a crooked grin and approaches you. . . .

Now let me ask you, who are you more willing to buy the Ferrari from? What if the salesperson in the plaid suit gave you half off? What if he handed you the car for free? Would you take it?

Sometimes discounts are a good thing. If the salesperson from the first scenario offered you 10% off, you'd be pretty happy, right?

Not all offers are created equally, nor are all environments. In trading, we need to learn how to interpret both.

There are many kinds of analysis we can do to help us interpret the trade and the environment it's in. We'll get into the details of each soon. But for now, know that we can perform fundamental analysis, technical analysis, and even psychological analysis. I've seen and experienced many approaches and combinations of these types of analysis in my day, gathering data and being dialed into the news, and listening in on the earnings conference calls. Even reading and trying to interpret the finer details of 10Ks may work extremely well for some but not others. That's okay. There are many ways to trade successfully. I'll share with you exactly what has worked for me and the thoughts behind it soon.

The truth is that there really is no one best approach. Some may lean a little heavier on one type of analysis than another. That's okay. I've studied many of the best traders in the world and have even been blessed to work directly with and befriend some of them. With that research and having helped thousands of traders globally, I can say with confidence that the three critical parts of any analysis we do are:

1. That it's proven to lead us to the results we're after;
2. It aligns with our beliefs; and
3. We're able to execute it well.

Trades and markets have similarities. We want to assess both the trade that we're taking (be it a stock, cryptocurrency, commodity, futures contract, etc.) and the environment we're buying it in. For example, if you bought NFLX at $390 as it was beginning to break out to fresh highs after the Covid bear market of April 2020, you would have been buying strength and buying in a great market environment. Sure, if you read the news at the time, the world was still falling apart, Covid deaths were on the rise, and lockdowns said to be two weeks were now more than two months. With most of the world stuck at home, it was a perfect time for Netflix to thrive. The stock nearly doubled in about a year and a half reaching a high of $700 by November 2021. See the chart below (see Fig 2.3).

FIG 2.3

Other stocks such as ZM and PTON moved even more during this time period. ZM's price ran more than 450% in eight months. PTON ran about 350% over a similar period. Both fit the broader narrative of the world being on lockdown. Zoom enabled many people to video conference with each other and work from home. While Peloton brought virtual spin classes into the home. Both existed before Covid. Both saw their demand skyrocket when people couldn't leave their homes. See the charts of ZM (see Fig 2.4) and PTON (see Fig 2.5) below.

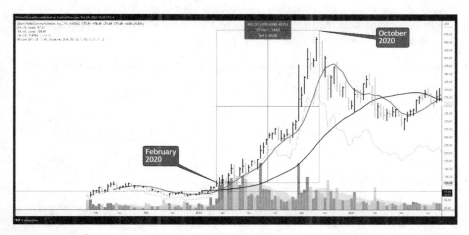

FIG 2.4

FIG 2.5

We'll review the finer details of how to go about finding stocks like these. For now, the idea is to identify trades that match the environment we're in.

Fast-forward to the present day. I'm writing this section on May 25, 2022. NFLX is now trading at $186. A bargain? Maybe. Was the Ferrari in the vacant lot a bargain?

Presently we're in a bear market, which started in November 2021. At one point, NFLX was down 50% from the peak of $700 (see Fig 2.6). Was the stock a bargain at $350? Well, remember the story from earlier and how I traded that airline parts supplier? From $350, NFLX dropped by another 50% and at one point was trading at $175. Was that a bargain? How about when it dropped even further to its present low a few weeks ago of $162.71?

FIG 2.6

This highlights one of the major psychological problems with trying to pick a stock's low price or what's often referred to as "bottom fishing." When we bottom-fish, our premise for buying gets better as the price moves lower. "If it was a bargain at $350, it must be a steal at $175, right?"

Maybe it bounces, maybe it doesn't. Maybe the price trades in a range between $175 and $200 for the next few years. If you were planning to simply buy and hold, your money would be going nowhere. At that point, you might be better off buying an index fund such as SPY or QQQ. At least you'd be diversified.

Trades and the markets affect each other so much that there's often a debate about which is more important. At times, it can feel like a "which came first, the chicken or the egg" scenario. The reality is they are both important, and they both play a role. Our job is to develop a systematic way to analyze both.

INFLUENCES AND STUDIES

I think there are two major junctures in our trading. The first is when we are new and in discovery mode. We don't know what we don't know, and we're figuring out what we like, what works best for us. If you're in this stage, give yourself time. There were plenty of times throughout my personal journey when I was in a rush to get to the end. If I had had perspective on this discovery stage back then, it would have saved me quite a bit of angst.

Once we figure out the style we like, we can go much deeper into its rabbit hole. That's what happened to me after I read *How to Make Money in Stocks*. I began reading similar works and tried to gain different perspectives on what the author was teaching.

Even when we learn and like something, questioning our beliefs and keeping a beginner's mind enables us to create the mental space needed for us to evolve. Our environment and the influences we allow in it play a major role in how we evolve.

I've had many trading influences throughout my life, some positive, some negative, some life-changing.

I'll share my top five trading influences with you now. Each has had profound impacts on my trading and my life. I wouldn't be on the path I am now if it were not for their influence. They are:

1. **William O'Neil** (*How to Make Money in Stocks*): Foundational. O'Neil taught me the basis for developing a systematic approach in the market, to wait for the right time to enter, to cut losses short, and to let winners run.

2. **Nicolas Darvas** (*How I Made $2,000,000 in the Stock Market*): My inspiration for trading part time. Darvas was a ballroom dancer who traded part time in the 1950s. He did his work at night and on weekends. He drew charts by hand.

3. **Van Tharp** (*Super Trader*): My first formal introduction to trading psychology. Tharp taught me that "we don't actually trade markets. We trade our beliefs about the market." His work inspired me to develop trading plans and business plans and gave me new insights into position sizing.

4. **Stan Weinstein** (*Secrets for Profiting in Bull and Bear Markets*): I gained a deeper understanding of trend analysis from Weinstein and how to more effectively stick with winning trades by using a combination of moving averages and price structure.

5. **Mark Minervini** (*Trade Like a Stock Market Wizard*): All I had learned about trading previously was fine-tuned and turbocharged when I discovered Mark Minervini's work. I learned about the finer points of chart patterns, timing, and the mathematics behind developing super performance.

FUNDAMENTAL ANALYSIS: DEFINING OUR UNIVERSE

I like to think of trades and the criteria I'm using as being like a funnel with multiple filters. There are about 10,000 stocks in the market. While many of them might be capable of producing the results we're after, we only want to consider the ones with the highest probability of doing so. By narrowing our focus, we greatly improve our odds of success. Having been through the full Investor's Business Daily course load and been an IBD Meetup Leader for nearly a decade, it may come as no surprise that the tactic I use for narrowing my focus is derived from William O'Neil's CANSLIM.

I'm a student first. The art of mastery is one that involves continuous learning. While I may consider O'Neil to be one of my biggest influences, a student with only one teacher lacks perspective. Having had multiple teachers, I've adopted the Bruce Lee philosophy of Jeet Kune Do, taking what works, and leaving the rest behind. This has led to a custom-fit version of trading for me. I encourage you to custom fit your trading as well, especially as your trading continues to evolve. The custom-fit version of trading that I've come up with for myself is what I call E.A.G.L.E.

As the name might suggest, E.A.G.L.E. stocks are the types of stocks that can soar! Each letter of the acronym E.A.G.L.E. stands for the qualities that when combined lead to a higher probability of it being able to soar.

Extraordinary earnings, sales, and/or projections;

Asymmetric high probability, high reward to low-risk opportunities;

Game Changers, Groups, and Growth

Leadership: market leadership, group leadership, leadership within groups;

Environment: the overall market environment.

There are only about 200–400 names in the US stock market at any given point in time that fit these E.A.G.L.E. criteria. I'll take the stocks that pass this set of baseline criteria and move them onto a special watch list that I refer to as the Universe List.

Stocks can enter into or leave my Universe at will based on the E.A.G.L.E. criteria. **I'll never trade a stock that is outside my Universe.** This one sentence alone has saved me thousands of dollars and untold amounts of time. In doing this, we've already narrowed our focus between 96% and 98%.

Entering the Arena and Finding the Stocks Ready to Play the Game

To whittle our list further, we need to come up with a well-structured weeding out process. Essentially, there are two things for us to consider:

- The minimum criteria to enter the arena;
- The minimum criteria to play the game.

Regardless of our trading style, we're not going to be interested in every trade out there. The market is an infinite stream of opportunity. In order to capitalize on any of it, we need to pick our spots.

The criteria we select must be aligned with the outcomes we hope to achieve. As Albert Einstein once said, "If you judge a fish by its ability to climb a tree, it will live its whole life believing that it is stupid."

So, for example, if we are aiming for high-octane trades capable of making 50% or even 100% or more in a few months, we shouldn't consider ones that are slow and pokey, and vice versa.

Personally, I'm interested in these high-flying, high-octane kinds of trades. So I'll use these as the examples here in this book.

A Universe of E.A.G.L.E.s: The E.A.G.L.E. Criteria

As mentioned earlier, there's no need for us to reinvent the wheel. A large part of why I've found success using my system is because it's built off the work of others who have had success before me. I've simply molded it into a custom-fitted design for myself. Since this custom-fitting process is one of the secret ingredients to success, I highly recommend you take what is presented here, learn it as-is first, and then custom-fit it to your liking. Make it your own. Install the beliefs that lead you closer to your goals. Leave the rest behind. Elevate your game.

Now let's walk through the finer details of E.A.G.L.E.

E: Extraordinary Earnings, Sales, and/or Projections

As the name suggests, we're not aiming for average or even pretty good. We're aiming for something extraordinary! Something that will help us filter the market (approximately 10,000 stocks) down to the top 2–4%. That means in the strongest of market environments I'm reviewing approximately 400 names. In a weak environment, it's cut in half to only about 200. How do I know if the environment is weak or strong? In part, through following this screening process. It's the screening process that tells me how many stocks are fitting the criteria. Breadth counts. If you were to walk into a grocery store and the shelves are fully stocked, it's a good time to buy. If the shelves were empty, like during the height of Covid, it's not.

I find it best to screen for stocks that have at least one of the following characteristics. The more of these it has, the better:

- Accelerating earnings for at least two quarters;
- Accelerating sales for at least two quarters;
- Earnings of at least 25% for the three most recent quarters;
- Sales of at least 25% for the three most recent quarters;
- Forward earnings projections of 50% or more for the next quarter;
- Forward sales projections of 50% or more for the next quarter;
- Earnings % growth of at least 25% for the past three years;
- Earnings % change of at least 50% for the most recent quarter; and
- ROE 17% or higher.

There are several tactical screens I like to run when building the Universe. I'll often focus a screen on one area at a time flipping through stocks manually to see which ones I want to add to the Universe. This semi-automatic process gives me the best of both worlds. I'm not screening through 1000s of stocks every week, just a few hundred. I'm only seeing ones that are potentially Universe-worthy. And I get the tactile feel that can only come from manually reviewing them.

If you would like a free PDF of the specific screening criteria I use, go to tradingmindwheel.com/resources.

When defining the rules of the game, we often think about what to include. When it comes to trading, it's also a good reminder that anything that doesn't make it into the rule set isn't included and is therefore a distraction. For example, you may have noticed that I didn't include the PE ratio as part of my screening criteria. It's not something that I've found to be particularly useful in weeding out E.A.G.L.E. stocks, so I've eliminated it. The PE of a trade I'm interested in could be 500 (as in the case of NFLX back in 2010), or it could be in the teens. It doesn't matter to me either way.

A: Asymmetric High Probability, High Reward to Low-Risk Opportunities

We want to come up with definitions for high-probability trades and ways to define when something is low risk and high reward.

The way that I determine whether a trade is a high probability setup is based on the following:

- The chart pattern;
- The price and volume activity within the chart pattern;
- The current market environment;
- How closely it fits my full E.A.G.L.E. criteria.

When a trade opportunity crosses our field of vision, it's easy to get swept up in the moment. It may look great to us, and we feel excited! Conversely, if we're coming off a string of losses, we might be skeptical of an otherwise great opportunity.

Seeing if all the stars align on a trade when we're in a great mental state can still be confusing at times. While a basic checklist can help and be a good start, I've found that problems arise when multiple stocks end up checking off the same number of boxes. Then what? Do we buy them all?

To help view trades more objectively and intricately, I developed a tool that I call the Trade Gauntlet.

I like to make each trade I take "run the gauntlet." This Trade Gauntlet is essentially a weighted average checklist of all the criteria I'm interested in. By putting every trade that I'm interested in through the gauntlet, it helps me to make sure that the trades I'm considering actually do fit my criteria, and it helps to remove any psychological biases I may have had at the time. I've found it exceedingly useful as a double check that a trade meets the criteria I'm interested in. It also helps stave off "itchy fingers" as my friend, former client, and current Mara Coach Stuart Chalmers likes to say.

You can try out the Trade Gauntlet for free or you can build your own. Go to tradingmindwheel.com/resources to try out the Trade Gauntlet.

So how do we actually know if a trade is high reward and low risk?

There's a variety of ways you might calculate this, but essentially the question is, How large of a return are you expecting relative to how much you plan to risk?

For example, suppose you bought a stock at $100. How far do you antici-pate that this price might run and over what length of time? If you're a swing trader like me, you may anticipate the price to run from $100 to $120 within three to six weeks, giving you a 20% gain. If you're a day trader, you might be looking for a move of a few dollars but are only planning to hold it for 30–90 minutes. This is your reward.

The other side of the ratio is the risk. Where do you plan to cut your loss if price moves against you? Historically I cut losses at around −5%, so if price fell to $95, I'd likely be out.

So in this example, I'd be hoping to make $20 while risking $5. My reward-to-risk ratio would be 4:1.

Personally, I always want the reward-to-risk ratio to be skewed in my favor. I want to be getting odds on my money. If I'm getting 4:1 odds on a trade, I could lose three times in a row, win on the fourth, and still come out ahead. There's obviously a *HUGE* advantage to this. We don't have to *rely* on a high winning percentage to make money. The key word here is "rely." Could we have a high batting average? Sure. But do we want to rely on a high batting average to make money? Why not give ourselves the best odds for success by not relying on a high win rate? If we're getting 4:1 odds, we can win half the time and be way ahead.

G: Game Changers, Groups, and Growth

This is where some of the art of fundamental research comes into play again. The stock's story comes into play. Is the company dynamic? Is it changing the way that we live, work, and play? Does it fit the present narrative of the market?

There's quite a bit of subjectivity in each of those questions, right? It isn't black and white. There are many shades of gray. It's for this reason that the ego can sometimes get wrapped up in the decision-making process. Often traders feel that they know the company. They believe in the story. It has historical precedent. These are all common arguments I've heard for entering trades, holding trades for big moves, and sometimes holding trades for way too long and giving back significant gains or watching trades turn into losses.

One experience I had witnessed with a stock's story being the near downfall of a friend came in the 2007–2008 financial crisis. At the time many of the large banks were thought to be too big to fail. A friend believed this story and bought Citigroup at about $10/share. Believing in the story, he rode the stock down for more than a 50% drop. Two years later the stock eventually climbed back and he sold for near breakeven. As a new investor, this was gut-wrenching for him.

Art and subjectivity can have their place in trading for some, but this requires a lot of skill. Developing those skills comes with time and experience. But even then, having rules and developing the discipline to follow those rules is what keeps us safe from ruin. My friend had neither and was quite lucky to have gotten out with his shirt on.

Here's an example of how understanding the story can work out favorably. At the time of this writing, Russia and Ukraine are at war. Several months before the war started, stocks in the energy and agriculture sectors were set up and broke out. Some made huge runs of 20–70% in only a few weeks. Some of the ones I personally traded were CF, NTR, CVX, MUR, EQT, and KOS, just to name a few. See Fig 2.7–2.12.

FIG 2.7

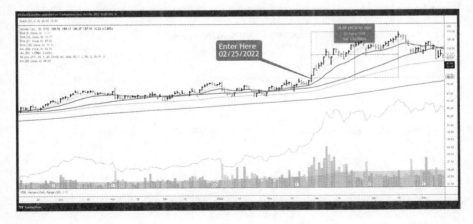

FIG 2.8

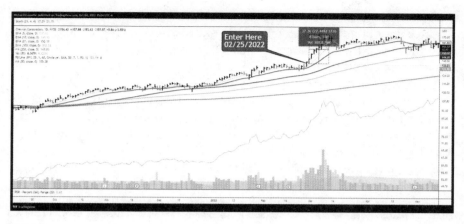

FIG 2.9

FIG 2.10

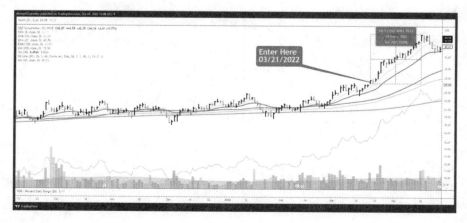

FIG 2.11

FIG 2.12

Stocks often move in herds, and when a group gets moving it can lead to large sustainable moves. The leaders in the group will often move a few days to a couple of weeks ahead of the rest of the group. This is why it literally pays to watch the setups and take note of when multiple stocks set up within the same group. And if we miss the initial breakout, it's okay because leading stocks will often offer multiple entry points. We may need to wait a few weeks for that to happen, but they do occur. Keep a lookout.

The other part of "G" is Growth. I'm looking for growing ownership and a minimum ownership by management of 10%, particularly within the first few years after a stock has IPO'd. This tells me that management is more aligned with shareholders and is more likely to behave in a way that favors shareholders.

The reason why institutional ownership is important is because it is primarily their buying and selling that moves the stock price over long periods of time. They can't enter and exit positions like individual players can. Everything is a double-edged sword. Institutions can influence price, but they're very slow moving. It takes them weeks or months to build positions and acquire the number of shares they wish to own. Individuals can often buy full positions in an instant with a single click. A great analogy that Mark Minervini uses is to think of the institutions as giant cruise ships and individuals as jet skis. We may not be able to influence price, but we can maneuver quickly. We can enter and exit at will.

There have been times in the recent past when individuals have gotten together and have been able to behave like an institution. Most recently this occurred with WallStreetBets, a group on Reddit, that collectively created short squeezes in the stocks GME and AMC. It's rare for individuals to effectively gather together and collaborate in this magnitude, but this is the power of the Internet, and this is why price pays. It's also why risk management, sizing, and all of the skills we discuss in this book are so important. Numerous hedge funds blew up due to not respecting risk. If we drop a boulder into the water, it makes a larger splash than dropping a few rocks. But if we take tens of thousands of rocks and drop them simultaneously into the water, it can have a similar effect to dropping the boulder. That's what happened with WallStreetBets.

L: Leadership: Market Leadership, Group Leadership, Leadership within Groups

A stock showing leadership qualities is of the utmost importance to my style of trading. Leaders move the most. If we're interested in making large gains quickly and turning over an edge, we want to trade the leaders. Leaders can come in three different forms.

Market Leadership: Market leadership is when a stock is outperforming the market and the broader indexes. We can tell that this is happening by looking at the stock's Relative Strength (RS) line versus the S&P 500. If it's moving up and to the right, there's a good chance it's outperforming the market. However, we also want to take note of the RS line versus the price action of the stock. Is the RS line outperforming price? If it is, this is a very strong sign. How is the RS line over the past 52 weeks? Is it at or near a 52-week high? If it is, that's another sign of market leadership.

Let's take a look at the charts of the prior examples to drive home the point. This time we'll highlight the RS line at the time of breakout and throughout the move. Observe the RS line in CF, NTR, CVX, MUR, EQT, and KOS (see Fig 2.13–2.18).

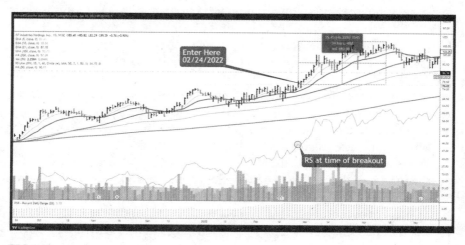

FIG 2.13

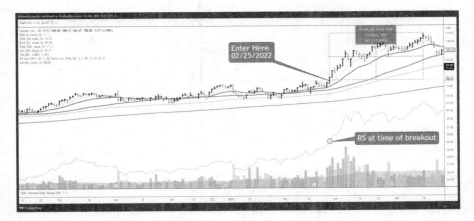

FIG 2.14

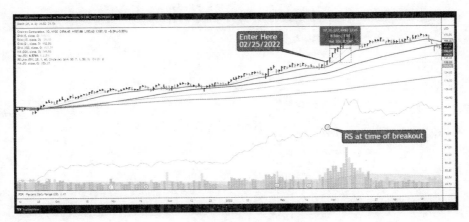

FIG 2.15

FIG 2.16

FIG 2.17

FIG 2.18

Group Leadership: Is the stock within a leading industry group or sector? Is that group or sector showing signs of improvement? Studies show that 37% of a stock's move is directly tied to its industry group. Another 12% is tied to its sector. Therefore, we want to pay close attention to the industry and sector that a stock belongs to. There are a few ways that we can tell when a group or sector is heating up.

First, we can assess the group's and sector's performance relative to the rest of the market. We can analyze the group and the sector's performance over the past week, month, quarter, and year. We can track its movement up and down the list as well as how they're moving relative to each other. There are a number of tools and resources available to help us do this. Yes, many of them are free. There are a few that I think are worth paying for and have done so. To see all of these resources and to learn more about them go to tradingmindwheel.com/resources.

Next, look at your own Universe of stocks. There's a wealth of information here! Did more stocks from a certain industry group or sector come onto that list this week, this month, this quarter? That's an important sign. By way of our regular screening process, the market is telling us which groups and sectors we should be paying closer attention to.

As we run through our Universe list looking for the setups we're interested in, is there a significant number of stocks setting up from a particular sector or group? Are they setting up in a particular way? Often when a group or sector is getting ready to move, I'll find numerous stocks setting up together and forming similar patterns. This occurs often and happens in waves. It's also true on the downside. When we see numerous stocks from the same group or sector breaking down, more soon follow, and other related groups may follow in the next several weeks or months as well.

This is another clue. The sector or group with a sudden increase in the number of setups in it might be getting ready to move.

Leadership within Groups: A stock could also be a leader within its own group. Usually, there will be two or three leaders within a particular group that are far above the rest based on their earnings and sales, price performance, or both. What will happen is that each will take their turn leading the way. Leaders outperform. Therefore, my personal preference is to stick with the leaders.

The Trifecta of Group Leadership

Having one of the above qualities is enough to enter the arena. Having two is phenomenal and worthy of extra attention. While we don't always get all three simultaneously, when we do we want to pay extra close attention. As we attempt to stack the odds in our favor, confluence across all three leadership qualities is special. At the same time, we don't want to overvalue leadership to the point where we're making management errors. More on that later.

E: Environment: The Overall Market Environment

We have a whole section on analyzing market environments, so we won't go into too much detail here. For now, understand that studies show that three out of every four stocks will follow the overall trend of the market. While this is true, we want to be careful here. A common mistake is to wait for the market to turn before going long or before going short. That's what I used to do, and my performance suffered because of it. Some people might call this the "tail wagging the dog."

Leading stocks lead. Leading stocks will break out ahead of the market and will break down ahead of the market. Makes sense, doesn't it? I'm grateful to Mark Minervini, who pointed this out to me years ago. It's for this reason that when we consider market conditions, or what I refer to as "market mood," we want to take into account not just the indexes but also the leading stocks within them and, as we'll soon discuss, putting even greater weight on the stocks themselves.

DEFINING OUR SETUPS

Clearly defining what we're looking for in a trade gives us the clarity we need to move with precision and speed.

Our setup is the thing that causes us to execute the trade. Everyone who trades or invests uses setups, whether they are aware of it or not, whether they are clearly defined or not. Those who are not aware of what their setups are tend to be clumsy in their execution.

For example, consider the person who says, "Setups are bologna!" Okay, fine. An idea crosses their desk. It piques their interest. They buy. No setup, right?

Actually, in this case, the setup was a combination of an idea coming from somewhere and this person being interested in it. With about seven billion people in the world, I imagine this will work for someone. But I think we can do a lot better than this.

Part of how I define a setup is that it must first be from within my Universe. If an idea falls outside of my Universe, it may look pretty, but it's not a setup for me. If enough of these attractive ideas find their way into my consciousness, I may need to amend the definition of my Universe. That's okay, it's part of evolution. We are free to do so. However, any definition we amend should be done so deliberately, consciously, and with intent. If we decide to create alternate universes for different asset classes, we can. We can have universes based on strategies, tactics, and time frames as well.

Clearly defined setups help us increase our odds of success and help save us a boatload of time. For example, a stock chart is one of the primary parts of what I look at when considering a setup. I can glance at a chart for a millisecond and tell if I want to do more work on it or not. It's taken time for me to develop that kind of speed, but it all starts by having a clear definition of what I'm looking for. By knowing what to look for, we know what to add and what can be eliminated.

When it comes to defining and analyzing setups, we want to identify, model, and focus on the very best. A common error people make is thinking we should hunt for and identify flaws. There's a time and a place for identifying flaws, and we'll get to it. But for now, as we build our parameters, anything that doesn't make it in automatically counts as either irrelevant or a flaw.

Here's an example of what I mean. Book value is one of the more traditional fundamental metrics. According to Yahoo Finance, book value is "the total value that would be left over, according to the company's balance sheet, if it goes bankrupt immediately. In other words, this is what shareholders would theoretically receive if a company liquidated all its assets after paying off all its liabilities."

You may have noticed that book value was not a part of E.A.G.L.E. at all. So as far as my system goes, it's irrelevant. Maybe you agree. Maybe you disagree. For some, it may be one of the most important criterion there is. If that's the case, they should be including it in their system. Remember the customization process we mentioned earlier? This is part of how we put customization into action. Book value may not be something I find particularly useful, but if you do, go ahead and use it.

Start with the end in mind, and let it guide you on how to get there.

Remember the example we used earlier with the GPS in the car? How once we plug in the address, the GPS is able to guide us over, around, and through to get us to our destination? My destination is triple-digit annual returns. Sometimes I reach my destination. Sometimes I don't. Sometimes I even surpass my destination. Because I know my destination, I'm able to better select the vehicles to get me there.

Personally, I prefer stocks that can go up 100–1,000% within a couple of years or less. And it may sound odd, but I'm not even looking to capture the entire move. The reason why is because I don't need to. These types of stocks tend to have explosive movements, and getting odds on our money becomes a lot easier.

For example, let's say I'm looking to make a 10% minimum on a stock trade. I can buy a blue chip mega-cap stock that moves an average of 1–2% per day in either direction. I may be able to get to my 10% target, but the process will be long and drawn out. I want stocks that can move. That have oomph! A slow-pokey stock may get to the target but not in the desired amount of time. I'd never hit my triple-digit annual return objective this way. It's the same reason why you don't find anyone racing a tractor in NASCAR. They just don't belong.

To define our setups, I've found it helpful to come up with a template that we can fill out. This way, we can be sure that we check all the boxes and that we're not missing anything.

Setup Definition Technical Template

- **Name of Setup;**
- **Time Frame(s);**
- **Length:** Bars needed (minimum and maximum);
- **Depth:** Percentage drop from the top (minimum and maximum);
- **Look/Characteristics:** your personal description;
- **Placement within the Trend;**
- **Requirements to Trigger an Entry (breakout levels, support placement, % stop, targets);**
- **Market Type Needed for Trade;**
- **Models (3–5 examples of great ones).**

Our setups are what allow an idea to move from our Universe List onto our potential trade candidates lists. They take what was able to make it into the arena and allow it to play the game.

The types of setups I personally trade the most are:
- Pullback Buy;
- Cup with Handle;
- Flat Base;
- High Tight Flag.

These account for more than 80% of the trades I take and are more than enough to get you started. If you'd like more, check out the resources over on tradingmindwheel.com/resources.

Within each of the setups I look for, there are certain common characteristics I like to see across the board. They include volatility contraction, dry-up in volume on the right side of the base, net accumulation within the base, high relative strength, and the major moving averages (21 ema, 50 sma, and 200 sma) trending higher. As I'm flipping through charts, I've trained myself to be able to spot these characteristics at a glance. If a trade lacks them, I move on immediately. If it has them *and* is one of the above setups, it will get added to a "Trade Ideas" list.

Examples:

- **Name of Setup:** Pullback Buy;
- **Time Frame:** Visible on both weekly and daily time frames;
- **Length:** Bars needed (minimum and maximum) 7days-5wks
- **Depth:** Percentage drop from the top (minimum and maximum) 10–20%;
- **Look/Characteristics:** Typically pulls into the 21 ema or 50 sma with a slope of about 45 degrees; the price action should be smooth and controlled; volume typically dries up as we move further to the right of the chart;
- **Placement within the Trend:** Up 1x or more the range of the original base;
- **Requirements to Trigger an Entry** (breakout levels, support placement, % stop, targets) support to be established at the 50 sma or 21 ema; a positive reversal bar at those levels; a shakeout + positive reversal is a plus; 2–4 days of sideways action;
- **Market Type Needed for Trade:** Uptrend, Sideways, or IF found in a down-trending market, it must be close to a model setup OR market is close to bottoming / potentially turning;
- **Examples:** Zscaler Inc (Ticker ZS, Oct 2021) (see Fig 2.19); Charles River Laboratories International, Inc (Ticker CRL, March 2021) (see Fig 2.20); Paycom Software, Inc (Ticker PAYC, Sept 2021) (see Fig 2.21).

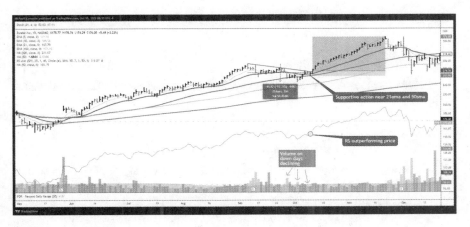

FIG 2.19

FIG 2.20

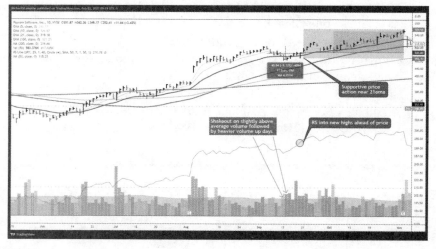

FIG 2.21

- **Name of Setup:** Cup with Handle;
- **Time Frame:** Visible on both weekly and daily time frames;
- **Length:** Bars needed (minimum and maximum) approx. 7–35 wks.;
- **Depth:** Percentage drop from the top (minimum and maximum) approx. 20–35%;
- **Look/Characteristics:** Think of a teacup with a handle; this base is generally U-shaped and has a handle at the end of it; the better handles appear in the upper half of the base, drift sideways or down slightly, and the volume dries up;

- **Placement within the Trend:** Continuation pattern within a stage 2 uptrend;

- **Requirements to Trigger an Entry:** Support to be established at the 50 sma or 21 ema; volatility contraction; three days of sideways action before breakout;

- **Market Type Needed for Trade:** Uptrend, sideways, IF found in a down-trending market, it must be close to a model setup OR market is close to bottoming / potentially turning;

- **Example:** XPEL, Inc, (Ticker: XPEL, July 2020) (see Fig 2.22); SolarEdge Technologies, Inc. (Ticker: SEDG, Dec 2020) (see Fig 2.23); Zillow Group, Inc (Ticker Z, May 2018) (see Fig 2.24).

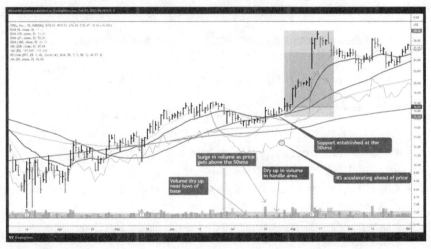

FIG 2.22

FIG 2.23

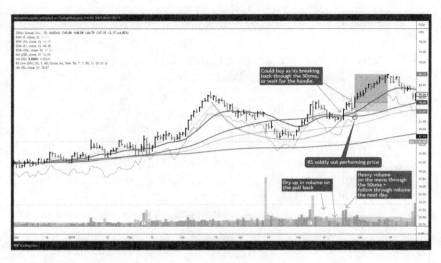

FIG 2.24

- **Name of Setup:** Flat Base;
- **Time Frame:** Visible on both weekly and daily time frames;
- **Length:** Bars needed (minimum and maximum) approx. 5–12 wks.;
- **Depth:** Percentage drop from the top (minimum and maximum) approx. 10–15%;
- **Look/Characteristics:** It looks like a rectangle; price action in the better ones tighten up toward the end;
- **Placement within the Trend:** continuation pattern within a stage 2 uptrend;
- **Requirements to Trigger an Entry:** Support to be established at the 50 sma or 21 ema; volatility contraction, three days of sideways action before breakout;
- **Market Type Needed for Trade:** Uptrend, Sideways, IF found in a down-trending market, it must be close to a model setup OR market is close to bottoming / potentially turning;
- **Example:** Donnelley Financial Solutions, Inc. (Ticker: DFIN, Oct 2021) (see Fig 2.25); Diamondback Energy, Inc. (Ticker: FANG, Dec 2017) (see Fig 2.26); Amazon.com, Inc (Ticker: AMZN, Jan 2018) (see Fig 2.27).

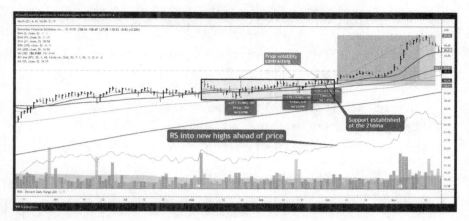

FIG 2.25

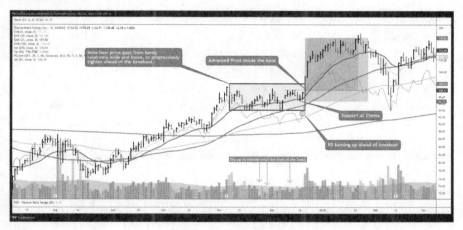

FIG 2.26

FIG 2.27

- **Name of Setup:** High Tight Flag;
- **Time Frame:** Visible on both weekly and daily time frames;
- **Length:** Bars needed (minimum and maximum) approx. 4–8 wks. for the pole w/ a move of about 100% or more; the flag should be a minimum of about 10 days and a max of 5 weeks;
- **Depth:** The flag portion should be no more than 30%;
- **Look/Characteristics:** There are two parts to the move, the pole and the flag; the best flags pull back on relatively low volume and get progressively tighter;
- **Placement within the Trend:** Continuation pattern within a stage 2 uptrend;
- **Requirements to Trigger an Entry:** Support to be established at the 10 or 21 ema; volatility contraction, three days of sideways action before breakout;
- **Market Type Needed for Trade:** Uptrend, Sideways, IF found in a down-trending market, it must be close to a model setup OR market is close to bottoming / potentially turning.
- **Example:** Shopify, Inc. (Ticker: SHOP, June 2020) (see Fig. 2.28); United States Steel Corporation (Ticker: X, Jan 2021) (see Fig 2.29); Astria Therapeutics, Inc. (Ticker: ATXS, Oct 2022) (see Fig 2.30).

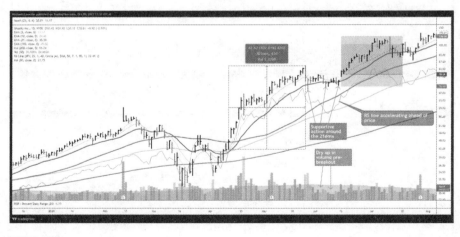

FIG 2.28

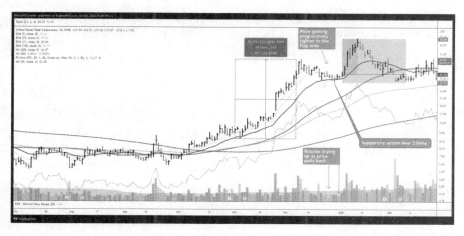

FIG 2.29

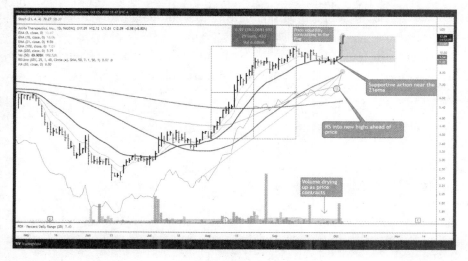

FIG 2.30

As I go through the Universe and look for setups, I'll build out a list of trade ideas. Both the quantity and quality of the setups we find are key determinants of what I call "market mood." If we're thinking of the Universe and we're flying through space in a rocket ship, do we have a clear path to Mars, or are we in the midst of a meteor shower? If we're in a fishing boat, are the fish practically leaping onto the boat, are we on the water the entire day without a bite, or somewhere in between? When we're out there on the water, what kind of fish are we catching? Are they large and lively? Are they smaller?

Are they keepers or ones you'd likely toss back? This is how we want to think of the market each time we run through our Universe List and look for setups.

DEVELOPING A FUNNEL

Now that we have our Universe and our list of setups, we want to develop a funnel. Our funnel helps us focus. It gets us from the Universe to our planet, from our planet to our country, and ultimately to the best spots to be in.

The way I like to break this funnel down is into lists and sub-lists. These include:

- **Universe:** All the trades I'm interested in;
- **Trade Ideas:** Ideas from the universe that are setting up;
- **In the Neighborhood:** Ideas from the trade ideas that are getting close but are not quite tradable yet; they could be ready this week;
- **Focus:** Ideas from the trade ideas list that are ready to go;
- **Action:** The ideas I consider best and I intend to buy (or sell short);
- **Open Trades:** Trades I'm in and am actively managing.

Focus is one of the major keys to success in anything. By funneling our lists down in this way, we're focused on the top 0.01% of trades in the market that fit our system.

ANALYZING MARKETS

Now that you've learned how to find great trade candidates, you need to learn how to analyze the market that we're in. Are we buying that Ferrari from the showroom or from that vacant lot?

There are many ways to slice, dice, and analyze market conditions. Basically what any of these methods want to do is zero in and let us know when the conditions are good, average, or poor for our style.

We started with analyzing trades because I found it to serve a dual purpose. Not only are we finding great trades, but also the quality and breadth of trades we find can give us great insight into the market environment.

Think about that car dealer. You walk in, it's clean, it's stocked. You're in the market for an electric vehicle. They happen to have the one you're interested in. And to top it off, the government just rolled out a new incentive program for electric vehicles. It's a great time to buy.

Conversely, what would happen if you showed up to that same dealer but the lot was empty and the attendant was putting a padlock on the gate? You couldn't get in. No one else could get in. No one is buying a car from this dealer today. It's not a great day to buy a car, is it?

The same could be said for your trades. If you run your screens and one day you find an above-average amount of setups and they're all high quality, you know it's a good time to get involved.

Conversely, if you run your screens and you come up empty or find only a handful of borderline trade ideas, you know it's time to sit and wait. We don't want to get in the habit of sacrificing quality for immediacy. If you find that quality trades come too far and few between, it doesn't mean that we should start moving down the quality ladder. It means that it may be time to add a new setup to your repertoire or see if your setup works in a different asset class or time frame.

Here is an outline of what I consider when sizing up market conditions or what I like to call "market mood":

- Trend analysis across the major indices across time frames;
- Distribution count over the past 25 days and over the past 10 days;
- Number of stocks making new highs versus new lows;
- Size of the Universe List;
- Size of the Trade Ideas List;
- Quality of setups in the Trade Ideas List;
- Performance of the Trade Ideas List as a whole;
- Performance of Open Trades;
- Performance of prior 10 trades.

In this way, I'm factoring in the market, my system, and my personal performance. This creates a Venn diagram such that where the center falls is how I define the current market mood. That center is simply green, yellow, or red. See Fig 2.31.

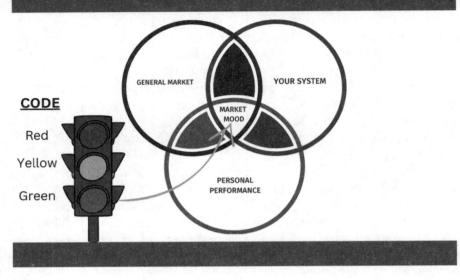

DEFINING MARKET MOOD

CODE

Red

Yellow

Green

GENERAL MARKET

YOUR SYSTEM

MARKET MOOD

PERSONAL PERFORMANCE

FIG 2.31

Part of the reason that assessing market conditions is so important is because it will help us size our positions more effectively. If conditions are ideal for our system and we find an ideal trade, we should be betting heavier. Even if we lose on that particular trade, it makes sense to bet heavier when conditions are optimal. Conversely, it makes sense to trade lighter when conditions are less favorable. Step on the gas when it's nice, sunny, and you've got a straightaway with no traffic. Go slowly when there's traffic, you're approaching a curve, or it's raining. The way to do this is to have a robust way of assessing market conditions.

Let's go through the various elements one at a time so that you understand them thoroughly and are in a position to begin researching them further.

Trend Analysis Across Time Frames

Here is where I'll look at the five major US stock indexes: the S&P 500, NASDAQ, Russell 2000, NYSE, and Dow. I'll observe them across time frames and assess their trends.

There are nine trend types. Dr. Van Tharp discusses them in his work. I've found viewing trends in this way to be useful and have adopted them. These nine market types form a matrix.

On one axis we have the trend (up, down, and sideways), and on the other axis we have the level of relative volatility (light, average, heavy).

Trend

up/light	up/average	up/heavy
sideways/light	sideways/average	sideways/heavy
down/light	down/average	down/heavy

There are two additional ways I've found to view trends that are helpful as well. Simply bullish or bearish. While these can be applied to all three trend types, I find them to be particularly useful for sideways trends.

Sideways trends are transitional. They can help us observe whether the sideways trend is developing a bullish bias and may soon transition into an uptrend or a bearish bias and is more likely to soon develop into a downtrend.

Below is a snapshot of how I assess these trends. (See Fig 2.32.)

FIG 2.32

When assessing trends in this way, part of what helps us determine the smoothness and likelihood for the trend to continue or end is the multi–time frame aspect of them.

It can be helpful to think of time frames as you would boats in the ocean. Your monthly time frame is a large cruise ship. The weekly time frame is a medium-sized yacht. The daily is a speed boat.

Picture each of these vessels moving through the water in the same direction. They're each making their own waves, but the current is smooth as they are all in line with each other.

Suppose the speed boat decides to see if it can speed up and move around the yacht and the cruise ship. Do you think it could? Sure! It could do so pretty easily, right? What do you suppose will happen as the waves from the speed boat cross in front of the yacht? It might get a little choppy, right? How about the cruise ship? It'd hardly feel the waves.

Now, what if the yacht all of a sudden decided that it too wanted to speed up and get around the cruise ship? Do you think it might cause the cruise ship to rock a little? I realize that it depends on the size of the yacht, but I think you understand the point.

Now, what if the speed boat encounters waves from the yacht? How about waves from the cruise ship? It may get airborne. It may even flip over!

This is what happens on the charts, and we can watch this play out right in front of our eyes.

Distribution Count over the Past 25 Days and over the Past 10 Days

I've found the distribution day count to provide another great clue into the condition of the general market as well. Coined by William O'Neil, a distribution day is a down day on an index of at least −0.2% or more on heavier volume than the day immediately before it. The significance of this is that as these distribution days pile up, a tendency may develop to cause uptrends to turn into sideways trends and sideways trends to eventually form downtrends.

What I've noticed is that the distribution day count has greater significance when looked at over the past 25 trading days as well as over the past 10.

Over the past 25 days: during this time period we can gauge the relative distribution on an index to prior short, intermediate, and long-term corrections. We can judge what's normal versus what's abnormal.

Over the past 10 days: during this time period when we see the distribution count climb above four, it forms what's known as a "distribution cluster." Selling is particularly heavy during this period and may cause the market to roll over.

Alternatively, when we see the market in a downtrend and the distribution count begins to lighten, it's one signal that pressure has been somewhat alleviated and that a new rally may be around the corner.

Number of Stocks Making New Highs vs. New Lows

As far as conditions go in the stock market, the number of stocks making new highs versus the number of stocks marking new lows is often the "canary in the coal mine" so to speak.

To borrow another quote from my friend Mark Minervini, "We're not just looking at the 'stock market,' we're looking at the market of stocks." If the market of stocks is showing that more and more stocks within it are making fresh highs, in the short term wouldn't that make it more difficult to fall?

On the flip side, if the market is going to fall and keep on falling, wouldn't we see the number of stocks making new 52-week lows also increase?

This has played out so well time and time again that it has become one of my go-tos when assessing market mood.

Here's a chart of the NASDAQ with the number of stocks making new highs versus new lows below it. The first chart (Fig 2.33) is from January 2018 to February 2019. The second chart (Fig 2.34) is from September 2019 to September 2020. The third chart (Fig 2.35) is from October 2021 to September 2022.

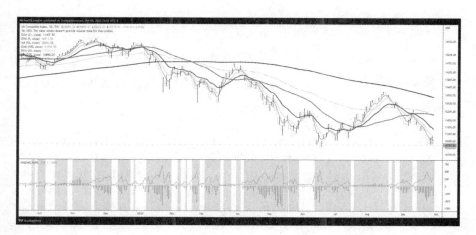

FIG 2.33

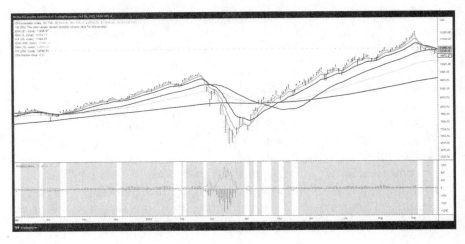

FIG 2.34

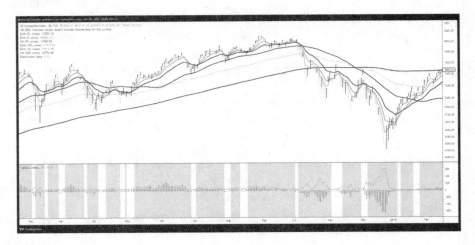

FIG 2.35

Take note of the transitional phases in each of these. Before each downturn, the number of stocks making new highs dries up while the number of new lows expands. On each major downturn, the number of new lows expands further, while the number of new highs remains low. Before the upswings, the number of stocks making new lows dries up, and the number of new highs begins to expand. On the upswings, the number of stocks making new highs increases while the number of stocks making new lows remains low.

If this were a steakhouse, the first group of indicators would be the side dishes that complement the meal. This next group of indicators helps you customize how you want your steak cooked.

Size of the Universe List

Consider the universe of stocks that you're interested in. All these stocks have passed your unique set of parameters. Is that list growing or shrinking? At what rate is it growing or shrinking? Let's think about it for a moment: if there are more and more stocks that are passing our criteria, that's a good thing for our system, isn't it? That means that there are more possible opportunities. Wouldn't the opposite be true if fewer and fewer stocks passed our criteria?

When fewer and fewer stocks pass our criteria, what many people do is switch the criteria so they can get more opportunities. After all, if we're trying to fish in a pond with no fish, shouldn't we switch ponds?

That's how I used to think about it, and it lead me to do what is often referred to as "system hopping."

While it's true that we wouldn't necessarily want to trade a system that works great in uptrends but loses money in downtrends, ignoring the system completely would be folly. We can often get some great information from that system. For me, part of it comes in the form of monitoring the overall size of the Universe List.

We could go far deeper than that. For example, we can look into the sectors and groups being added to or removed from the list.

Size of the Trade Ideas List

In trading, size matters. I'm not talking about position size; we'll get to that later. I'm talking about the size of our ideas list. If we go through our Universe list and we find many of the types of setups that we defined as part of our system, then that's a sign from the market that it could be strengthening. Personally, I like to take a look at the number of stocks in each sector and group that are setting up as well. Often when I find a number of stocks within one sector or group setting up, it's an indication that the sector or group is getting ready to move too. Being that my system is designed to look for leading stocks, I'm often able to find a group or sector move just as it's starting to happen.

Quality of Setups in the Trade Ideas List

The quality of the setups we're finding can tell us a lot about the market too. If we're finding a large number of "A" level setups that are showing everything we like to see and are offering a great level of reward to risk, then this is telling us that based on our system the environment has improved. Conversely, if the setups we find are mostly trash, even if we have a large number of trade ideas, the market is telling us that we may be scraping the bottom of the barrel and to be on the lookout.

Performance of the Trade Ideas List as a whole

As we continue to dig deeper into our own lists, we can see how the trade ideas list performs as a whole. Is it positive or negative for the week (or the period you've made it for)? How far have the winners moved? How about the losers? The way that the market treats the stocks that are setting up for us tells us a lot about the relationship between our system and the current environment, and provides us with insight into how aggressive we should consider being. If 70 or 80% or more of stocks are positive, it's like shooting fish in a barrel so to speak. On the other hand, if only 20% of stocks are positive on the week, that shows that our chances of picking a winner have dropped substantially. It doesn't mean that we shouldn't trade per se. But we should incorporate this kind of feedback into our decision-making process.

Performance of Open Trades

One of the best indicators of the market mood can be our performance within it. If we've done everything previously discussed, are focused on and taking only the best of the best trades, and are executing every other part of our system and we're still not making progress, then the market may be ready to roll over. This has been one of the keys that helped me switch stances from bullish to bearish at key junctures. Most recently as of the time of this writing, on June 9, 2022, near the open I was stopped out of the remaining long positions I had on. Taking that plus the other market factors into account, I saw that it was a great time to begin testing the short side. I sent an alert to our members. The market then proceeded to fall about 10% over the next three days! (See Fig 2.36.)

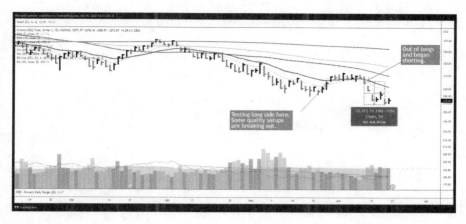

FIG 2.36

This isn't luck. This is what happens when skill, preparation, and opportunity meet. You can 100% develop these skills for yourself.

Performance of Prior 10 Trades

Knowing our stats is important and has a variety of applications. If you're new, expect your win rate to be a little erratic. Kind of like baseball. If you're just learning how to hit, you'll lack consistency at first. However, as you gain more and more experience, not only will you improve, you'll also start to see what your win rate typically is. For me, it's about 45% over the long term. What this tells me is that if I start to fall below that, the market conditions may not be great for my particular style of trading and I should be more cautious. If I'm doing particularly well, I may consider pressing a bit more if other factors line up too. Knowing my stats has saved me a fortune over the years.

RISK: Initial Capital Risk, Position Sizing, Potential Reward

If this is your first time hearing about risk, then it might very well be another four-letter word. However, when it comes to trading, how we manage risk is critical. It's one of the reasons why when we discussed mindset earlier, we included a variety of exercises around money and your beliefs around money.

One of the things that can happen in trading, especially in the beginning and at major life junctures, is that our systems are not in alignment with our true risk appetite. That is the amount that we are truly comfortable with losing if we're wrong.

When trading, the risk in a trade is one of the costs of doing business. As Stuart Chalmers likes to say, we've got to pay to play. The initial risk we accept when putting on a trade is the amount we're willing to pay.

This goes hand in hand with our arena example from the prior section where we are the referee and the trades are the competitors. The initial risk is their entry fee to compete. How much should each competitor pay to compete in the arena?

There are a few ways we may think of this cost:

1. Dollar amount;
2. Percentage amount;
3. Slice of the pie (could also be calculated as a percentage of total capital).

Rather than falling into one camp only (I did that for years), I find it best to consider all three so we get the best perspective.

Suppose you're starting out with $100,000. You decide that on the next trade you take, you don't want to lose more than $1,000. This is equivalent to 1% of your capital.

This does *NOT* mean that you only would buy $1,000 worth of shares. You could potentially go all in with your full account (not recommended if holding overnight) and the moment the price moves 1% against you, you can exit the trade with a loss.

In this example, that $1,000 represents both your initial capital risk and the maximum you're willing to risk on this trade.

Now suppose you found a trade where you could enter at $100, and it would make sense on a technical level to exit the trade if price fell back below $95. You'd be risking $5/share. You could then purchase up to 200 shares and keep to your maximum desired risk of $1,000, or 1% of capital. In this instance, it also equals 20% of your account. This is your position size.

Now let's suppose you had another rule, one that said that you'll allocate no more than 25% of your total starting capital to a single position. You're good in your first trade, but what happens if another trade pops up where you can enter at $200 and exit based on a technical stop of $195? You're still risking $5/share, but this time that $5 only represents a 2.5% risk between your entry price and where you would exit with a loss. In this case, you could theoretically purchase 200 shares, but your size would be 40% of your total capital.

You decide that's too much and want to keep your size to 25% of total capital as you had originally planned. You reduce the number of shares you buy to 125. Now your position size is 25%, but the amount of capital at risk is only 0.625% of your original $100,000.

This is how math can really work in your favor. As your risk amount gets smaller (presuming you've adhered to all that we've discussed so far), you can potentially make more money faster. This is how you cap your downside risk. We'll get into the other part of the equation, the reward side, soon enough.

To help you understand the math, here's the formula that I used to calculate these sizes. You can take the formula and put it into a spread-sheet. Or you can use the free position size calculator we've created. Go to tradingmindwheel.com/resources for access.

(Total Capital × % Capital Risked) / (Entry Price − Exit Price) = Number of shares to buy.

Try it for yourself with the inputs from the earlier examples.

Our primary objectives as far as capital risk, potential reward, and position sizing go are as follows: Look for asymmetric opportunities where rewards are high relative to the risk. Size in such a way that the risk of ruin (i.e. blowing up our account) never occurs.

RISKS INVOLVED IN RISK

When we think of risk in trading, many thoughts may come to mind. There's a risk of losing the trade. There's a risk of being wrong or doing something incorrectly. There's also a risk of losing money. Each of these risks is part of trading. We can do our best to mitigate each of these risks, but at the end of the day they are all a part of the game, and if we're not okay with that, then we shouldn't be trading.

Now here's something I think is worth mentioning. There's a difference between being okay with these risks while trying to mitigate them, and not truly being okay with them and trying to mitigate them. Here's what I mean. When I first got serious about trading, after I had found O'Neil and even after I had begun talking with Avi, Rich, Curt, and Jim, I wasn't truly okay with any of the aforementioned risks. I thought I was, but I wasn't. I was unaware and had not learned about mindset yet.

You see, it's one thing to check a box on a form that says, "I'm okay with these kinds of risks," the kind of form many financial advisors or brokerages may provide. It's quite another when we're actually confronted with these risks. All types of fears can kick in. If we're starting from a place of awareness, we have a fighting chance. If we're not aware, it'd be like a random person off the street trying to box Muhammed Ali in his prime. It wouldn't end well.

The primary three risks we'll focus on here are the risk of losing money, the risk of being wrong, and the risk of losing on a trade.

Risk of Losing Trades

It didn't take me too long to figure out that I wasn't going to win every single trade. It did take me a while to learn that there's a difference between a winning trade and being right.

You see, it's possible for us to win a trade and be completely wrong. We could get lucky and hit the jackpot once, can't we? We could also close our eyes, walk across the street, and be perfectly fine. Does that make it a good idea? Could we do either of those things, hit the jackpot, or walk across the street with our eyes closed and be okay consistently? Of course not! There are many people who have gone broke trying to win the lottery. There are plenty of people who have been struck by cars and killed.

To alleviate the fear of being wrong in a trade, first, we must perform the exercises in the mindset chapters. After that, we need to redirect our focus. As in most things in life, we need to focus on the things we want, not on avoiding the things we don't want.

For example, if you're driving down the road and suddenly lose control of your car, the focus should be on regaining control of your car, not on avoiding the telephone poles. The reason why telephone poles get hit is because people are focused on avoiding them. They don't want to hit the pole and yet they're staring right at it. If they simply focused on the road and regaining control of the car, they'd avoid the telephone pole by default without even having to think about it.

The way to apply this to trading is to shift our focus from winning to process.

"But wait a minute!" you might be thinking to yourself. "You said to focus on what we want, and what I want is to win."

This is true. We do want to win. So the question then becomes, How do we win?

We win by focusing on the process of winning, not the outcome of winning. Here's another example to help drive home the point. If you wanted to drive across the country, would you stare at the GPS or would you occasionally glance at it to make sure you're on track, but keep your eyes on the road the other 99% of the time?

When Michael Jordan, one of the greatest basketball players in history, was in the game, where do you think his focus was? On winning or on doing what needed to be done in order to win? If he was looking at the scoreboard all game long, he'd be focused on winning but would have ended up losing because he wouldn't have been focused on the processes that would lead him to win.

In trading, what we must focus on in order to win is executing our system flawlessly. Do you think it's possible to do that? It may sound like a tall order, but let's break it down.

Do you think you could execute your system flawlessly for one day? What would need to happen in order for you to execute your system flawlessly that day? Write down whatever comes to mind.

Here are a few things that help me execute my systems flawlessly each day.

1. Pre-flight checklists: In the morning, often before the market opens, I'll reread my notes from the evening before. I'll read my thoughts on the market and the trade management notes I've written on my open trades. I'll also review the notes I've made on any trades I'm planning to take that day. In doing this, my mind is clear, and I know exactly what I need to do.

2. Pre-landing checklists: Toward the end of each trading day, before the market closes, I'll check each of my open trades and see if any danger signals are appearing. Depending on the number of danger signals I see, I'll take action. If there's no action required, I'll sit with my open positions.

3. Disembarking checklists: After the market is closed, I'll assess the market's mood. Based on these assessments I'll then make any necessary adjustments to the trading plans on my open trades as well as any trades I'm planning to take the following day.

I'll repeat this process and focus on executing it flawlessly each day. The more I've made this my focus, the better I've performed. I'm not perfect, far from it. Life still throws curveballs, and I do my best to adapt.

One of the best ways to adapt is to have adaptation, or contingency, plans set ahead of time.

What happens if the power goes out? What happens if your broker has problems and can't execute? What happens if there is a family crisis? How about a natural disaster? These things may not be fun to think about, but it's better to think about them on our time rather than being caught in the middle of them without a plan, isn't it? Take some time now to think about these questions. Write down your answers. Flag this page. Do what you have to, but make sure you develop these plans.

Here's how I've handled these problems:

- **Power goes out:** I have apps on my phone for each of my brokers and have trained myself how to use each of them well;
- **Power goes out *AND* phone battery low:** I carry a backup charger and cord with me during the trading day;
- **Broker has problems and can't execute:** I have accounts at several brokers; if one goes down, I can place temporary hedges in another;
- **Family emergency or natural disaster:** I always have stop-loss orders on every open trade; at the absolute worst, those stops keep me safe from ruin.

And if anything arises that causes my judgment to be impaired, there are contingency plans for that as well. If no one else can manage our account for us, we can have a plan to exit positions and not place any new ones until our minds are right.

Contingency plans aren't just for the negatives or life's curveballs. We should have them for positive events as well. I learned this lesson the hard way.

Melissa and I got married on April 30, 2011. It was a gorgeous Saturday afternoon, and everything was perfect down to the smallest detail. The church, the flowers, the limo, even coming up from the floor like rockstars to "Welcome to the Jungle" at the reception. Months and months of planning, and everything went off without a hitch.

We left for our honeymoon the Monday after. We flew from New York to Honolulu. With a brief stop in Chicago, the trip took us about 15 hours in total.

During this time I had a trade on in SLV. I entered the trade on February 14, 2011, at about $30. In only two months' time, I was up about 60%. The Friday before our wedding, April 29, 2011, price had closed at $46.88. I was thrilled. The profits from this one trade alone would have more than paid for our honeymoon.

... That is if I had remembered to place a stop loss.

I didn't look at the market at all on May 2, the day after that, or the day after that. I didn't look at the market again until the Monday we returned from the trip on May 16. I opened my account and to my chagrin, SLV had dropped all the way back down to $33.82. In the span of two weeks, SLV had fallen by 30%. My +60% profit had turned into +10%. See Fig 3.1.

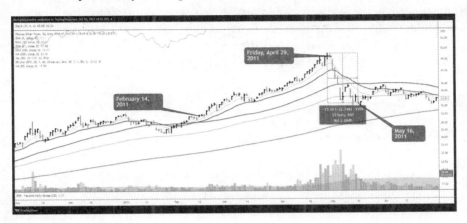

FIG 3.1

It was here that I learned to always have a "going away plan" for your trades. If you're keeping positions open, double-check that the stop losses are in place.

Risk of Being Wrong

Many people think being wrong and losing are the same thing. I did too at one point. But as I mentioned earlier, these are not the same.

Being wrong in a trade means that we are not following our system. We are not following our rules. If we do not have a system or rules, then by default everything we're doing is wrong. Without a system or rules, nothing is guiding our trades.

Think of it like this. Imagine you get in your car to drive, but there are no rules of the road. No traffic laws telling you when to stop or go. People might be driving on the opposite side of the road, on sidewalks, cutting through the neighborhood park to get to where they want to go a little faster. It'd be chaos.

We need systems and rules to follow so we know how to operate, so we can tell what is right and what is wrong. We can question these rules and systems as we evolve. We can make changes and upgrades. But without some standard by which to operate, we're in chaos.

Judge "right" and "wrong" by how well you follow your system and rules, not by the result of an individual trade. Great trades executed perfectly can sometimes result in a loss. Terrible trades executed in error can sometimes result in profits.

A basic system and set of rules are better than none at all. At least you'd be able to form a baseline and could journal your results. You'd have the opportunity to perform a post analysis (more on post analysis later) and see what parts worked and which ones didn't. Setting up a law to drive in one direction on one side of the road is a vast improvement to the society we imagined earlier.

Risk of Losing Money

The idea of losing money can go to two extremes.

1. We're absolutely afraid of losing any money at all;
2. We have a complete and total disregard for money and are willing to risk it all.

In the first case, money is so dear to us that even with a great system and rules it will be difficult for us to execute. The fear of losing is so great that it becomes a distraction in nearly every trade. In this case, we must work on our relationship with money. The exercises in the mindset chapters can help. Another exercise that can help is budgeting. Yes, budgeting.

I was surprised when I learned about this, but it helped to cure my fear of losing money, and it strengthened my relationship with it.

For years I had a massive fear of losing money. Not wanting to put me or my future family into a position where we could ever return to my early childhood days. Homeless and living in seedy motels. This fear of lack and fear of helplessness gripped me. I needed a rock-solid plan. Budgeting was the answer.

When we budget our money, we have a plan for it. We know where it's coming from, where it's flowing to. And great plans for wealth plan ways to grow money.

A great quick read for budgeting and developing a great relationship with money is George Cleson's *The Richest Man in Babylon*. If you haven't read it yet, then I highly suggest you do.

The part that applies so well for us here in trading is the principle of 10, 10, 10, and 70. It essentially goes like this.

As we get paid (from a paycheck, business, etc.) take the first 10% and put it aside for giving. Take the next 10% and set it aside for building something or selling something. Something that can generate revenue in the near term. Take the next 10% and use it for longer-term investing. That last 70% is what you use for personal expenses.

Done in this way, we are constantly earmarking money for different purposes. That 10% that we're using to invest or to build a business (perhaps a trading business as Dr. Van Tharp discusses) has a specific purpose and is not the same money that we'd use to keep a roof over our heads and our stomachs full. There's less emotional attachment to that money because we've given it a specific purpose.

MINDSETS NEEDED FOR RISKING CAPITAL

Cost of Doing Business

Think of the initial capital at risk in each trade as the cost of doing business, the amount required to see if the trade will be a winner or a loser.

Once we have a proven system, the way to keep our cost of doing business small is to focus on taking the best trades in the right environment. If we're taking mediocre or poor trades in a great environment, our cost of doing business will be high. If we take great trades in a poor environment, our cost of doing business will increase. If we are taking great trades in the right environment, our cost of doing business will be low.

Should we take great trades in a poor environment?

The answer: it depends.

What we should do is follow our systems and rules.

The system that I follow has me executing great trades regardless of the environment. If I kept my sizing constant (more on sizing shortly), my cost of doing business in a poor environment would naturally increase. To mitigate these costs, I discovered ways to gauge the market environment (discussed in SPOKE 2 on Analysis) and to adapt my level of exposure accordingly. This way I'm trading my largest when everything is lined up and my smallest when it isn't.

How Much Do We Want Our Costs to Be?

There are several ways to think about this question. Each of them leads back to sizing and where we will exit a trade if we're wrong. If, for example, we decide that we're willing to bet the farm and will allow the trade to go to zero, then our risk is 100%, and we risk getting knocked out of the game completely.

There are some people who will think about the tremendous gains that can be made from going all in. "What if the trade works out? What if it goes up 100%? 200%? We could very easily double our money! Even if it only goes up 20%, that's still huge! Think positive! That's what mindset is all about, right?"

Unfortunately this kind of "positive thinking" isn't really positive at all. It's oblivious and delusional, and it leads to blown accounts. In trading, we don't want to see things better than they are. We certainly don't want to see things as worse than they are either. We want to see things as they are. Trading too large inevitably leads to blown accounts.

See the table below. This table shows how much of a gain is needed to get back to even after sustaining a loss.

Drawdown % in Trading Capital	Return % to Get Back to Even
−5%	5.3%
−10%	11.1%
−15%	17.6%
−20%	25.0%
−25%	33.3%
−30%	42.9%
−35%	53.8%
−40%	66.7%
−45%	81.8%
−50%	100.0%
−55%	122.2%
−60%	150.0%
−65%	185.7%
−70%	233.3%
−75%	300.0%
−80%	400.0%
−85%	566.7%
−90%	900.0%
−95%	1900.0%

With losses of only 5% or 10%, getting back to even isn't so bad. However, once we get beyond that point, the math really starts to work against us, doesn't it? Even at just a 25% drawdown, we need 33.3% to get back to even. At a 40% drawdown we need 66.7% to get back to even.

My personal single largest percentage gain ever in a trade came in Dogecoin. I purchased it on 02/23/2021 for $0.04779 and sold it on 05/21/2021 for $0.43, giving me a whopping 799.77% gain on the trade in only three months. Even with this kind of percentage gain, if I had gotten myself into an 85% drawdown, I would just be getting back to even. If I had a 90% drawdown, I'd still have another 100% to go!

Hopefully, this illustrates the point well enough for you to keep your losses small. The secret sauce to winning long term in trading is compounding our gains. Compounding is how we can build a sizable fortune. One of the keys needed for that to happen is to keep our losses small and by *NEVER* taking any trade so large that it knocks us out of the game. Even if we are 99.9% certain that a trade will triple our money, we never want to risk it all.

What Are the Risk Requirements of the System We Want to Use?

There are two kinds of risk in any trading system: risking capital and risking time. We need to figure out what our personal comfort levels are for each and what level is required of the system we're going to trade. Our personal comfort levels and the levels required for the system we're going to trade must be aligned. If they are not aligned, we're going to run into problems.

For example, remember when I told you how I first discovered O'Neil and fell in love with the CANSLIM methodology? How everything in the book made perfect sense to me and how my plan was to follow everything Bill wrote in *How to Make Money in Stocks* to the letter?

Well, unfortunately, that didn't work out too well for me at first. The reason in part was my risk tolerance in both time and money was different from his, and I discovered this the hard way. Even though his methodology works and produced a massive fortune for him, and even though *most* of his methodology worked for me, this one ingredient being misaligned threw the whole recipe off.

You see, O'Neil would aim for massive returns. Stocks that could go up several hundred percent in a few months or a year or so. I liked that part. However, what came with following his method to the letter was having to sit through basing periods. A stock could be up 50–60%. To follow Bill's method completely, we need to sometimes sit through a pullback of 25% that could last for a couple of months. I learned the hard way that I wasn't comfortable with that. It took me about a year to learn why and figure out some solutions.

Here are a few of the reasons I discovered why I was personally uncomfortable with Bill's method of risk tolerance.

1. Many times a stock wouldn't just pull back 25–35% but would pull back even more, and I'd give up a large gain;
2. I'd lose time, sometimes as much as two months while a stock consolidated;
3. A double whammy (stock breaks down further AND loss of time);
4. Other stocks on my watch list moving higher without me while I'm waiting for this one to consolidate.

Do you see some of the problems I was running into here? Do you see the dilemma of holding views like these can have on executing a system that doesn't match? By not having these perspectives ahead of time, I spent a year struggling with a system that I actually liked.

Luckily I didn't do what a lot of other people do in this position (and frankly what my younger self likely would have done), which is toss the system completely and start again from scratch. When we find something we like, it's worth seeing if we can tailor it to fit us better.

Making these adjustments on our own and testing them is one way to do it. Another is to study others. One of the great things about trading right now is that so many of these stylistic permutations have already been tested. We'll go into detail on this in the chapters on Testing. For now, we can see how others are doing what we want to try, and learn from them. It's often just a few clicks away.

Take a few moments here to answer these questions for yourself:

- How much capital am I willing to lose in a single trade?
- How much of a percentage loss (distance between where you enter and where you'll cut a loss) am I comfortable with in a trade?
- How much of a gain am I comfortable giving back?
- How much time am I willing to sit in a trade both when it is moving in my favor as well as when it's going sideways or going down?

Your answers to these questions may or may not be entirely clear right now. Your answers may change over time. Both are okay and perfectly natural. We'll want to revisit these questions on a regular basis. Write those questions down in your journal or flag this page so you can come back to it easily.

When to Pull the Plug?

Knowing when to pull the plug on a trade is important. Knowing when to pull the plug on a system is also important. The easiest way to figure out the answer to both is with a little math.

Let's go back to the chart from earlier.

Let's say that we're in agreement that finding a stock that can go up just 5–10% is pretty easy. Using the chart from earlier and comparing the two columns, you can see that the difference between them becomes greater than 10% at the 30% drawdown level. At a 30% drawdown, it takes 42.9% to get back to even. Beyond that, the mountain to climb back up gets even steeper. Knowing that and preparing for it by keeping losses small can save us a fortune and keep us in the game!

If we have a rule that says if we lose a max of 20%, we pull the plug and reassess, we need a 25% gain to get back to even, a difference of 5%. This is doable.

Clawing our way back to even may not be fun, but it's better than getting knocked out completely.

Here's an example from a test account I had where I dug myself into a massively deep hole. If you're just starting out, I don't recommend you do this. Even if you have experience, following the above −20% max rule will save you a lot of time and money. I did not have to allow this deep of a drawdown to know that what I was doing wasn't working.

Over the span of about a year from July 2018 to August 2019, I had allowed my test account to drop about −97%. Embarrassing? Yes. Horrendous? Definitely. Completely unnecessary? Absolutely. But it did provide me with a great example to share with you here and to also share what's possible.

Here's a snapshot of the account:

At first glance, you may notice a few things:

- The size of the account is pretty small, it's under the Pattern Day Trading (PDT) rule in the United States;

- It took less than a year to get back to even;
- Within about 15 months I was able to run the account up +14,871% off its lows.

What led to the initial drawdown was a combination of failed tests and a disregard for the overall risk to the account. I just kept testing away, running similar strategies. Because I viewed the starting balance (only about $3,000) as barely a drop in the bucket, I didn't care about the losses. This was a huge mistake! Not because it resulted in blowing up the account, but because I had opened the door for a very bad habit. Habits have a way of bleeding into other areas. In this case, other areas of our trading and potentially other areas of our lives.

With only about $90 left in the account, I finally decided that the tests I was running weren't working (ya think?), and it was time to try something else. I decided to see if my swing trading strategy (outlined earlier in the analysis section) could work for day trading options.

As it turns out, that strategy worked out extremely well for me. In less than a year, I grew the account by nearly +2,000% and was back to even.

At the time, my mind was blown. I had read about percentage returns like this but hadn't dreamt I could actually do it. People in books did that. People winning investing championships did that. Certainly not me. At least that was my belief at the time.

All of the fears and doubts of this being a fluke, about the actual dollar amount being small, and other thoughts related to imposter syndrome swarmed my mind. I could have allowed myself to believe those thoughts. Thanks to meditation and the various beliefs and self-development exercises mentioned earlier, I came to understand and appreciate that we are not our thoughts. We are the consciousness of thought. We can choose to believe or not believe whatever we want. This disassociation from thought created enough space for me to let go of those negative thoughts.

Do negative thoughts still pop up in my mind from time to time? You bet! Do I still occasionally stumble? Of course! In doing all this work, we stumble less, but perhaps more importantly we learn how to pick ourselves back up when we fall.

Here's something that may surprise you. Soon after that +2,000% climb and getting back to even, I put that strategy on the backburner!

WTF? Why on earth would I do that?? And what about the other +12,000%? How'd that happen?

Here's why and how.

It was February 2020, and life had begun changing for me once again. Covid hit, and the world was moving into lockdown. Trading was great. The markets never closed. But the rest of the world was seemingly spiraling out of control. I wanted to do my part to help. Unfortunately, there was little else I could do while using this style of day trading. It consumed much of my time, and while in a trade, it required 100% of my focus for the duration of the trade. I couldn't so much as go to the bathroom lest a full gain could quickly turn into a loss. I wouldn't be able to effectively run the strategy and do what I saw as my part to help.

Thankfully I didn't need the additional income from this strategy to live on at this point. My family and I were comfortable. I knew I had this strategy in my back pocket anytime I needed it. Plus, and perhaps more importantly, I learned once and for all that no matter how bad things got or would ever get, no matter how big of a hole I was in I could always climb back out. That homeless scared little boy from 34 years ago was now a very capable man who is able to provide for himself and his family. The key factors in making it happen were having a great system that aligned with my beliefs, goals, and ability to execute. That there is the magic formula.

So if the day trading strategy didn't produce the rest of the +12,871%, what did?

Swing trading crypto did!

Between February 2020 and November 2021, I adapted my swing trading strategy once again. This time applying it to crypto. I caught several major moves in Bitcoin, Ethereum, Litecoin, and Dogecoin. Many of the same rules and principles were applied. Similar sizing strategies were applied as well.

Part of what changed was how I managed risk.

Crypto is a 24-hour market. I had no intention of staying up all night to actively monitor my accounts. At the time, the crypto market was extremely volatile. Daily swings of 10–20% were common! Even with swings like that, the same technical patterns discussed in the analysis sections still applied. There are still times when volatility dries up. Price moves into a stage 2 uptrend. And trading breakouts from a Volatility Contraction Pattern (VCP) carried relatively little risk.

What changed for me was the following:

- Instead of risking 1% I allowed myself about 2.5% of capital to be at risk;
- I got aggressive and allowed up to 50% of my account to be in one currency at a time;
- I took breakouts that were only close to major support that I saw happening in real time;

- I gave trades more time to work (allowing them to sit on or around breakeven for up to three weeks);
- I sold into strength later, often at 2–3x my risk and only small portions; this allowed more of the position to compound;
- I aggressively sold the moment danger signals arose.

Doing all of this allowed me to generate +14,871% in a span of 15 months. Clearly, how we manage risk is huge!

WAYS TO EFFECTIVELY MANAGE RISK

Here's a great way to think about risk. Risk is what we stand to lose if we're wrong. Plain and simple.

Risk comes in three major flavors:

1. Capital;
2. Percentage;
3. Time.

Remember earlier when I shared that I didn't really care about losing trades in the test account? The flaw in my thinking was that I was looking only at the capital in the account, $3,000, which was a very small amount for me, and so I completely disregarded the percentage losses. This led to the blow-up.

In trading, it's possible to lose swiftly. It's possible to lose gradually. And it's possible to lose over a prolonged period of time. Our objective here is to limit losses in all three areas.

To do this, we can plan ahead of time how much risk in each area we're willing to accept *BEFORE* executing a trade.

For example:

Suppose we have a $100,000 account and want to risk a max of 2.5% of capital ($2,500) on a particular trade.

If we decide that we want to allocate 25% of our portfolio to any one trade, then we also know that we'll be putting $25,000 into the one trade.

Pretty easy so far, right?

Now let's say we found a trade where our entry price is $100 and our technical stop could be placed at $95 (if this were the case in real life, tactically I prefer to place my stop a few cents below the whole number. To keep the math simple, we'll stick with $95).

So we're risking $5/share.

Given the example, how many shares can we buy?

If we purchase 500 shares, we'd hit our max risk of $2,500. However, our position would be too large at $50,000 (remember, in this example the most we wanted to allocate was $25,000). So what do we do?

In this case, we can cut our risk in half. Instead of purchasing 500 shares, we can purchase 250 shares. Our total capital allocation is $25,000. Instead of risking $2,500 we are now only risking $1,250.

Remember, the *MOST* we wanted to risk was 2.5% of capital. This doesn't mean that we *HAVE TO* risk 2.5% of capital. All else held equal, each time we lessen our risk, the more favorable our reward-to-risk ratio can be.

Reward to Risk

Think of the reward-to-risk ratio as a seesaw. Do you remember those from when you were a kid? I was a pretty small kid, and I'd hang out with kids that were much bigger than me. I'd sit on it first. Then my larger friends would get on, and I'd be launched into space.

This is the kind of relationship we want when it comes to reward and risk. We want our potential reward to dramatically outweigh our risk. This gives us the chance to launch our equity curves into space.

Cutting Losses

Continuing with our seesaw, have you ever sat on one of those things and had the other person suddenly get off? What would happen? The first time you probably fell on your behind while the other kid laughed, right? Don't worry, it happened to me plenty of times, too. Eventually, I learned to be ready for my buddy to pull this and to put my feet down ahead of time to cushion the fall.

This is basically what cutting losses is like. We want to cushion ourselves lest we bust our behinds.

When it comes to trading, if we don't cut our losses, it'd be the equivalent of falling backward, hitting our heads, and being rushed to the hospital, unable to play again for a considerable length of time.

So how do we know when to cut losses and put our feet down on the trade? There are a few ways to do it. I like to use a combination of the following:

- Mathematical stop;
- Technical stop;
- Time stop.

Mathematical Stop

I consider a mathematical stop to be a certain percentage distance below my entry price. For example, cutting our loss at 5% if a trade moves against us is an example of a mathematical stop.

What we don't want to do is to pick a mathematical stop out of thin air. I tried that for a long time, and it failed miserably. When I was first learning O'Neil's system, I was introduced to the idea of cutting losses at a maximum of 7–8%. I naively took this to mean that if I entered at $100 I should always place a stop at about $93–$92. While I was indeed cutting losses faster, I learned the hard way that this isn't optimal.

Take our seesaw example, and picture a really tall kid with long legs on one side, and our other really big friend on the other side.

What if we told our tall friend that he or she could only place his or her legs at a certain height? He'd get a pretty nasty whack, you know where, that he wouldn't like too much.

This is the problem with using a constant mathematical stop. It doesn't always fit the trade. Better to think of a mathematical stop as a max and to think of that max based on the system we're trading.

My maximum stop is −10%, which is a factor of my average gain.

In this equation we always want the seesaw to be tipped in favor of reward, remember? Ideally, it should be a 2:1 reward-to-risk ratio or better. My average historical gain per trade is about 20%. If I cut losses at 10% max, I maintain my 2:1 reward to risk. See how this works?

Let's take it one step further and refer to the drawdown chart. I've reproduced it here for you.

Drawdown % in Trading Capital	Return % to Get Back to Even
−5%	5.3%
−10%	11.1%
−15%	17.6%
−20%	25.0%
−25%	33.3%
−30%	42.9%
−35%	53.8%
−40%	66.7%
−45%	81.8%
−50%	100.0%

Drawdown % in Trading Capital	Return % to Get Back to Even
−55%	122.2%
−60%	150.0%
−65%	185.7%
−70%	233.3%
−75%	300.0%
−80%	400.0%
−85%	566.7%
−90%	900.0%
−95%	1900.0%

If we lose once with a −10% stop, it will take us 11.1% to get back to even. Not too bad. Any more than that, however, and the math starts to work against us even more so on a trade-by-trade basis: −15% and we'd need a 17.6% gain to get back to even, −20% and we'd need a 25% gain. But if we're only averaging 20% gains on our wins, this becomes a big problem. Keep it up, and we'll go broke.

This is why we want to keep our losses as small as possible. As small as possible, that is, without going overboard. This is where technical stops come in.

Technical Stop

A technical stop allows us to put our feet down on the seesaw where it makes sense.

Take a look at the charts in Fig 3.2. My preferred method for finding a technical stop is to first look for tight, sideways action. A spot where price has visited, stopped, and has gone back in the other direction. This area is acting as a floor. If you're on the seesaw, this is the spot where you've been able to put your feet on the ground.

When setting a stop and cutting a loss, I like to look at the charts across time frames. The more time frames I can line up, the better.

Say we've got our big friend, our smaller friend, and our taller friend. They're all able to touch their feet on the ground somewhere. That spot is nice and firm. That's the spot we want to find on the chart, and the way we can do that is by doing a multi–time frame analysis.

Multi–time frame analysis may sound fancy, but it's as simple as looking at one time frame and seeing how it lines up with another. In fact, here's a snapshot of a trade I was in recently. Tesla, Inc. Ticker TSLA.

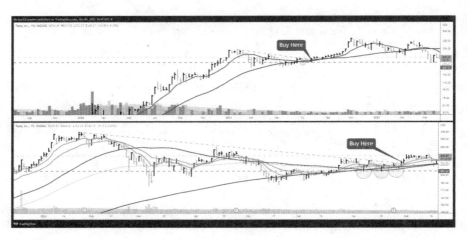

FIG 3.2

Here we have a weekly chart on top and a daily chart on the bottom. I drew the point of entry on both charts as well as a horizontal line where I'd place my stop and put it on both charts.

Do you see how price was progressively tightening up before the point of entry on both time frames? Do you notice how while the price was tightening up for a few weeks just before it was ready to break out, it was also bouncing from the same area around that horizontal line on both daily and weekly time frames? It was creating what's referred to as a "swing low." Swing lows can be great spots for a technical stop once the price breaks out of the range. The reason we want to see the price breakout of the top of the range first is because that is what confirms that the swing low is fully established.

Think of it like this: If you were to walk into a house and climb a flight of stairs, what was once the ceiling is now the floor. This is what happens with price. And as you're walking around on the second floor, you expect it to be nice and firm. In the market, sometimes we find that the floor isn't so firm, and that's what tells us it's time to exit.

So how can we tell when the floor is firm? We look for confluences: layers of time frames or other indicators that line up at or near the same spot.

There are at least two other technical spots that this stop happens to line up with.

The first is also on the daily chart. Take a look a little further back, and you'll see that the horizontal dotted line also touches a prior peak about a month back.

Seeing this is great, but ideally we'd find some more confluences that line up with this first spot we found.

If we look at the weekly chart above, you'll notice that it lines up perfectly with the weekly lows. Not only that, the peak from a month ago that we found on the daily also works on the weekly as well. Wonderful.

While it's still possible for the floor in a trade to fall out from underneath us, the more layers we can find to support it, the better. You may have noticed some squiggly lines on both charts. Those are moving averages. Price can also at times find support on or around the 50 sma (simple moving average) on the daily chart and the 10-week sma on the weekly chart. It's a confluence I often look for, and TSLA happened to have it.

We don't want to go overboard with indicators and technical analysis, nor do we want to throw in random factors that we're not regularly considering. If for example one day a friend tells you that price is getting supported at a Bollinger Band and you've never heard of it before, it shouldn't affect your view on the trade because it's something that falls outside of your system.

We can and should continue to learn and grow. If you hear about something and want to study it, you absolutely should. But only when it has been thoroughly vetted and has earned a spot in your system should it be allowed in. Otherwise, we'd be adding noise to our system. Throwing on random variables even if they sound good is the equivalent of trying to load up one side of the seesaw with random kids from the playground. It's not going to end well.

Time-Based Stop

The time-based stop gets us out of trades that are going nowhere. Think of the seesaw just sitting there. Not moving. We're not going to sit on this thing all night. Eventually, we had to go inside for dinner.

The time-based stop helps us know when enough is enough and to exit. There are a few ways to set this up. My preferred method is to use moving averages. Moving averages move with the price. So long as the price is above a moving average, the moving average will keep moving up along with it.

If you look at the daily chart from TSLA, you'll notice a squiggly line that is supporting the lows of the area we discussed earlier. That's a moving average. I like to keep a few moving averages on my charts to help me gauge momentum. Sometimes the price will bounce right off of a moving average. If, for example, price finds support at the 50-day simple moving average as it did here with TSLA, it tells us that for the time being, price is being supported.

The way for time-based stops to work very well is to figure out which ones you're going to use and to take trades that are near them at the onset. For my style of swing trading, I like the 21 ema most. This helps to keep me in the strongest short and intermediate-term trends. Sometimes, as was the case of TSLA, a variety of moving averages converge near the same spot. This is another way that confluence levels can be built and stacked on top of each other.

I prefer to take trades that are already near the time-based stop. If the trade doesn't work out, I don't have to wait very long to find out. If the time-based stop is triggered, I can exit and move on to the next trade.

Using All Three

Ideally, we want to be using all three on each trade: mathematical, technical, and time-based. Ideally, we want to have multiple time frames lining up as well. It's this cross-section that gives us the greatest significance and where we can have the most conviction.

Other Tactics, Pluses, and Minuses

There are other tactics and strategies that one may employ to manage risk, including the use of options, buying uncorrelated assets, buying inversely related assets, or shorting. The objective here still remains the same: mitigate losses and manage risk. Books have been written on each of these tactics. I'm not an expert on them, so I won't go deeper on them here. Go to tradingmindwheel.com/resources for more info. At this stage, knowing that there are additional methods available and where to learn more about them can be helpful to keep on the back burner. You can always learn more about them if the need arises. For now, keeping it simple is good.

Position-Sizing Methods

Position sizing is one of the most common places where traders get tripped up. Trade too large, and it only takes a couple of losing trades to completely blow ourselves up. Trade too small, and we can have a monstrous percentage gain, but it can have very little impact on our equity curve.

But what causes these problems? Where do they stem from?

Perhaps the biggest source is in a misalignment of beliefs and mindset. Here's a story of someone we'll call Gabe, who came to me a few years back wanting to make it big in the market. He grew up modestly in a two-bedroom apartment within a major inner city. His father left, and his mom was working two jobs to make ends meet. Occasionally in the winter, the furnace would go out, and he recalled having to heat the apartment by turning the oven on and leaving the oven door open.

Gabe saw himself as poor and was tired of being that way. He viewed trading as a way out. He logged onto Twitter and Instagram and saw people posting about how they made $5,000 a day, $10,000 a day, with just a few trades. Sit at the computer for an hour or two, and then hit the pool. No sweat! In less than a week these guys would bring home what his mom struggled to bring home in a year!

Gabe was going to get himself and his mom a better life through trading, or so he thought.

Gabe read a couple of books, a few of the ones I recommended to him including William O'Neil's *How To Make Money In Stocks*, Mark Minervini's *Think and Trade Like A Champion*, and *Trade Like a Stock Market Wizard*. He seemed enthusiastic and ready to get started. However, while he was enthusiastic about trading, he wasn't enthusiastic about the early results he was getting.

Was he losing money? No, quite the contrary. He grew his account by 10% in his first month! Phenomenal for a pro, let alone someone this early in their journey. However, since Gabe didn't have a lot of capital to begin with (he had saved up about $5,000 to start with) seeing an additional $500 in his account after a month of hard work wasn't enough for him.

"If only I had traded bigger . . ." Gabe told me.

"How big were you trading to start out with?" I asked.

"I put about $1,250 into each trade and risked about 1% of capital as you suggested."

"And look at the percentage return you achieved," I encouraged Gabe.

"Yeah. It's nice and all. But at this rate, it's going to take me forever to get me and my mom out of this apartment. I want to be rich, Mike! Just look at this . . . ."

Gabe took out some rough calculations he had done based on his return that first month.

1	$ 5,000.00	13	$ 15,692.14	25	$ 49,248.66
2	$ 5,500.00	14	$ 17,261.36	26	$ 54,173.53
3	$ 6,050.00	15	$ 18,987.49	27	$ 59,590.88
4	$ 6,655.00	16	$ 20,886.24	28	$ 65,549.97
5	$ 7,320.50	17	$ 22,974.86	29	$ 72,104.97
6	$ 8,052.55	18	$ 25,272.35	30	$ 79,315.46
7	$ 8,857.81	19	$ 27,799.59	31	$ 87,247.01
8	$ 9,743.59	20	$ 30,579.55	32	$ 95,971.71
9	$ 10,717.94	21	$ 33,637.50	33	$ 105,568.88
10	$ 11,789.74	22	$ 37,001.25	34	$ 116,125.77
11	$ 12,968.71	23	$ 40,701.37	35	$ 127,738.35
12	$ 14,265.58	24	$ 44,771.51	36	$ 140,512.18

"If I can keep up with making 10% per month, it's going to take me three years to make over 100k, and that's if I don't take out a single dime! I'm 23 years old. I want to go out and have some fun, too!"

"I'd hate to be the bearer of bad news, Gabe, but not every month will generate 10% returns. Some may be more, some may be less. There may be some losing months in there, too.

We do want to press things when the market is favorable for our system. That's the best time for us to make money. But no one system makes money all the time. Even if you average out to 5% per month, that would put you into the top 1% of traders in the world."

"Mike, I need money now. I don't want to wait."

"Is everything all right, Gabe? Are you being evicted?"

"No."

"Are you able to pay your bills?"

"Yeah, I always pay on time."

"Do you owe a bookie some money, and if you don't pay, they're going to break your legs?"

Gabe laughed. "No, it's nothing like that, Mike."

"Okay then. What's the hurry? This is starting to sound like the problem is lack of patience."

"I knew you were going to say that."

"Well, it's true. We may plant an apple tree and want to eat apples tomorrow. But no matter how much we want those apples tomorrow, the tree has to grow first.

Suppose we're not happy with that answer, so we're going to try to get the tree to grow faster. We give it twice the water and twice the fertilizer. What do you think would happen?"

"It'd grow faster?"

"No. We'd end up killing the tree before it grew at all. To get something to grow, whether it's a plant or our trading account, we need to give it what it needs to grow. Nothing more, nothing less."

"All right, fine. How about we just go to the store and buy some apples then?" Gabe said.

"Now there's an idea!"

"Huh?"

"If you want apples now, go to the store and buy some apples. If you want more money from trading, stick to your process. Produce consistent results."

"But Mike . . ."

"Let me finish."

"Okay, sorry."

"If you're able to produce consistent results, you'll get far more than just the money in your account."

"Okay, I'm listening."

"If you're able to produce consistent results, you'll build great habits and a great track record. It may not feel like it right now, but those are *FAR* more valuable than the money in your account.

For example, you can use that track record to attract investors. You know how hard trading really is. Most people aren't willing to put in the time and effort to develop the skills you're learning. Once you build up a track record of a couple of years, you'll be in a great position to get funded."

"A couple of years?" Gabe sighed.

"Yes, and that's provided you stick with it and continue building your habits, skills, and discipline. Be grateful if it's only a couple of years. Most professions take far longer with far greater tuition. Look at medical doctors for example. They study for 10 years between school, residencies, and internships. It's only after the 10 years that they start making any real money, and at that point, they often have hundreds of thousands of dollars in student loans to pay back."

"Geez! I hadn't thought about it like that before."

"I didn't either when I was in your shoes. But those are the facts. So are you willing to be just a little more patient and stick to the process?"

"100%. Absolutely."

"Perfect. Now let's review some sizing strategies."

Gabe's situation wasn't easy. He had a powerful why: wanting to improve life for himself and his mom. He had a growing skill set, early success, the perfect recipe to begin oversizing and blow up his account. Can you relate at all to Gabe? He was on the right track. He just needed some perspective to help keep him there, to help keep him focused on the process.

Remember when it comes to trading, it's easy to fall into the trap of trading too big or too small. We want to be like Goldilocks with our position sizes. They need to be "just right."

Two Styles of Sizing

I told Gabe, "When it comes down to it, we can break sizing down into two categories.

1. Fixed; and
2. Variable.

Fixed sizing can be thought of as what you were doing earlier, Gabe. You had equal slices of your account dedicated for each position. A variable position size just means that the size fluctuates."

"Why would we want the size to fluctuate?"

"Good question, Gabe. There could be a few reasons why. One reason could be that we're backing into size based on the amount we want to risk. Remember earlier how we talked about finding our entry/stop loss? Remember how we discussed risking a certain percent of our capital per trade?

Now with a variable size, you can take those three numbers and come up with the number of shares to buy. You can hold your risk constant but allow the size to fluctuate. For example:

Suppose you wanted to buy ABC and it was trading at $100. You identified support at $95 and placed your stop loss there. If you wanted to risk 1% of your capital and were starting with your original $5,000, you could buy 10 shares. Then $50 would be at risk.

1% of $5,000 = $50,

$100(entry) − $95(stop loss) = $5 risked/share,

$50(amount to risk) / $5(risked/share) = 10 shares.

Now suppose a few days go by, and now you're able to get an even tighter entry/stop: $100 is still the right entry, but the stop can be tightened to $97. Now we can buy 16 shares while still risking about $50."

"*Hey, the math works out to 16.7 shares. Why not round up?*" Gabe asked.

"You could do that. Over the long term though, I find it's better to be tighter with our risk for a few reasons. One, it builds a stronger habit of thinking about risk first. We want that. Think risk first, profits second. Profits take care of themselves, risk doesn't. We need to manage our risk, and as small as this habit may seem, it goes a long way in building our mindset.

Secondly, if we think back to that table of drawdown versus percent return needed to get back to even, the math works more in our favor the more we tighten our risk. We don't know which trades will be winners and which trades will be losers. If we make a habit of rounding down instead of up, we're allowing the math to work more in our favor over time.

That sounds pretty cool, right?

Here's something even cooler. We can combine both fixed and variable sizing and have an even stronger way to manage risk and increase our potential rewards!

So let's say you wanted to use 25% of your account on each trade. If you did this today, you'd be using $1,250.

In our first example where we'd enter at $100, set a stop loss at $95, we'd need to bump our capital at risk to 1.25% if we want to have a position size of $1,250.

Now for the sake of this example, let's say we're okay with the 1.25% capital risk. The math works to 12.5, but we're rounding down to 12.

Now suppose a few days goes by, and once again we're able to get a tighter entry and stop loss: $100 entry and $97 stop loss. We can keep our size constant at 12 while dropping our risk. Instead of needing to risk 1.25% of capital, we're now able to risk just 0.75% of capital while maintaining the same position size.

The reason we want to do that is because we're putting risk first. By keeping our position size constant and dropping the risk, we've tilted the odds of success even more in our favor. Holding all else constant, our upside targets remain the same; we're simply risking less.

So for example, if our target is $115, our reward is $15. Our reward-to-risk ratio R:R in the first case was 3:1 ($15 reward : $5 risk). In the second case, our reward-to-risk ratio jumps to 5:1 ($15 reward : $3 risk).

Now I ask you, with everything else held constant, would you rather risk $5 to make $15 or $3 to make $15?

You may be thinking this is a trick question, and it is obvious.

The answer is obvious now. Of course we'd prefer to risk less to make the same amount. But until we break the math down, most people don't think this way. I surely didn't when I was starting out.

I was focused on the reward side of the equation only. Risk was an afterthought.

Sometimes when things aren't working, taking a step in the opposite direction is the right direction. This turned out to be the case for me as far as sizing goes, and I haven't looked back.

Pyramiding into Positions

A lot of people ask me about pyramiding into positions. They read some books that suggest that rather than buying all at once when the price moves through the buy point, to buy in stages. So for example, if the price breaks out at $100, rather than buying all 12 shares, they'd start out buying half. Then as the price moves up, they'd buy the other half or even split that up and buy

30% and then the last 20% before the price got too much higher, say before $105 or so.

I think pyramiding into positions has its place, and if you're running a larger multimillion-dollar account, it can be useful. In this way, it affords the opportunity to see if price is breaking out and being sustained by buyers other than yourself. For example, suppose you're interested in a stock with a low float and low average daily trading volume. Suppose there are less than 100,000 shares traded on average per day and your account is $10 million.

If you wanted to enter at $100 with a stop loss at $95 while still using 25% of your account and risking 1.25% of capital, you'd be looking to purchase 25,000 shares.

For this particular stock, your buying would account for 25% of the average daily trading volume. If you attempted to buy all in one shot, you'd likely send the stock soaring and may not get filled near $100. You'd need to be more strategic with how you enter. To not send the stock up like a firework, soaring into the air quickly only to explode, you'd be better off using the pyramiding technique.

If you're starting out with a small account like Gabe, it's not a bad thing, nor is it a good thing. It just is what it is. I also know plenty of people who are new to trading, that have started with $10k, $100k, or even $1 million and learn trading the hard way. Isn't it better to start small?

So while trading a small account, why not use that to our advantage? We can enter and exit the market at will without having to worry about running up our average cost.

That sounds good and all, but what about when the trade turns around on us right away? Wouldn't it have been better to use the pyramiding strategy?

Sure! We can always find *SOME* cases when things would have worked out better had we done things differently. But that isn't the point. And if we get stuck in that kind of mindset (I was like that myself for ages), we can end up kicking ourselves each time something doesn't go our way. Instead of a trade generating a loss and its being just one outcome (which we already know is part of the system), we start taking it personally. Because we're responsible people. Because we know that we're in control of our own destiny. And because we know that part of creating the changes we want is by taking action, we start making tweaks to the system. But in reality, we're caught up in the minutiae. We're making changes from the wrong mindset and the wrong circumstances.

Whenever we're going to make any tweaks, we need to see how it will affect the whole. Everything has its price. Everything has its pros and cons.

We may get smaller losses with a pyramiding strategy in some instances. In others, we can actually have larger losses since our average cost is higher.

When we are trading a relatively small account (under half a million is generally considered relatively small) it's best to use that size to our advantage. Even at the $1–10 million mark, liquidity typically isn't *THAT* big of an issue most of the time. We do want to be mindful of the stocks we're trading. What's the float? What's the average daily trading volume? What's the spread between the bid and the ask (this is especially important when trading options)? If all of those are good, we're not in danger of turning the stock into a bottle rocket with our buying, then even with a medium-sized account of $10 million to under $100 million may not move the stock much. Think of the current mega-cap stocks such as Apple, Tesla, Meta, or whatever.

The point is that even if we have a $10 million account and want to put $2.5 million into Apple, we're not going to budge the stock. Right now it's trading at about $150/share. If we bought $2.5 million, it'd be 16,666 shares. This stock trades an average of 92.5 million shares per day!

And that's how liquidity can make a difference. In our earlier example, we'd be at 16.6% of the average daily trading volume. Do that in one shot, and you'll get a bottle rocket. With Apple, you're talking less than 1/100 of a percent.

Do you see how all of this fits together?

It's just like that bicycle wheel we talked about earlier. Right now you're in the process of putting on a new set of tires and inflating them. Pretty soon you'll have a nice smooth ride.

TRADE MANAGEMENT:
Managing Risk throughout the Life of the Trade

Give a trade every chance to work.

—Jim Roppel

As my friend Jim Roppel likes to say, we must give our trades every chance to work. Now, what do you suppose that means exactly?

To be honest, it took me a while to get perspective on this one. When I first heard it, I thought it was a reason to hold on for dear life (HODL). I took it to mean that if I could find a reason to hold on, then I should hold on. Well, as they say, "Seek and ye shall find." And finding a reason to do anything when it comes to trading is pretty easy.

Want a reason to buy? It's there. Want a reason to sell? It's there, too. Want a reason to hold? Look hard enough, and you'll find that as well. All we need to do is fire up our favorite search engine or social media platform, and we'll have plenty of answers right at our fingertips.

No, HODLing trades is not what Jim meant when he said, "Give a trade every chance to work." This is not what led to the extraordinary success he's enjoyed as a hedge fund manager, nor is it what led to his appearance in John Boik's *How Legendary Traders Made Millions*. No, when he spoke, he was speaking from a point of view that took into account much of what we've already spoken about in earlier chapters. He was not suggesting that we toss the rule book out the window. Rather, "giving a trade every chance to work" means that we strictly adhere to our set of rules.

Remember, *WE* are the game masters. We can have the power to develop all the rules to the trading game we want. If we've set the rules up in such a way that they actually do what they're supposed to do, why wouldn't we follow them all? Why wouldn't we give the trade "every chance to work"?

Whenever we exit a trade too early or even too late, we are not giving the trade every chance to work.

You might be thinking to yourself, "Wait a minute. If we exit the trade late, doesn't that mean we are giving the trade even more chances to work? We'll be in it longer after all. Isn't that better?"

I used to wonder the same thing. I learned the hard way many times over that giving a trade more chances to work than the rules specify is not better. Here's why.

It's kind of like cooking your favorite dish. We don't want to undercook our food, and we don't want to overcook our food. Both lead to indigestion. We want to cook our food for the right amount of time per the recipe.

Undercooked trades and overcooked trades are no good either. Each of them can cause financial indigestion. We want to hold our trades for the length of time that our rules specify. Then they will always come out to be just right.

Remember the game analogy? How in trading we are the game masters and perhaps the referee, not the player? The trades are the players. We need to give the trades every chance to work. Here are five rules in the trade play-book to help your trades go farther:

1. We only allow certain trades into the arena to begin with, trades that meet certain criteria.
2. We develop a set of rules for the trades to play within.
3. If the trades follow the rules, they remain in the game; if they break the rules, then they're out of the game.
4. As the referees, we must monitor the game to make sure the players (the individual trades) are playing by the rules.
5. As game masters, we must make sure the rules are leading to the desired result. If not, it's on us to tweak them. It's also on us to continuously review, update, and enhance the game. Even if the game is seemingly flawless, we must not leave staying flawless to chance. Checking in and making updates to a game allows it to evolve.

LIFE CYCLE OF A TRADE

Everything has a life cycle: markets, stocks, even trades. A life cycle includes a beginning, middle, and end. And like all things, life spans can vary greatly.

Whether we consider ourselves to be a swing trader or a day trader, a position trader or a long-term investor, we will all experience some trades that are shorter, some that are longer, and the vast majority will fall somewhere in between. They will all fall on a bell curve of sorts.

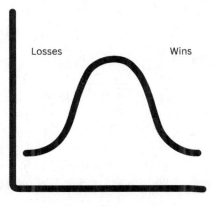

If we're trading well, our losses will be on the extreme left of the bell curve. We won't be in them for very long at all. Cut losses short, cut losses quickly.

Most of our wins will be average, somewhere in the middle. Our largest wins should fall on the far right of the curve as we hold them the longest and allow them to run.

Regardless of style, all trades come in three parts: a beginning, a middle, and an end. Thinking about them in this way is useful in getting a successful bell curve. Exit losers quickly. Allow potential winners to mature. Ride the biggest winners. And end with only the best of the best trades.

Now in order to do this, we must have a clear set of rules, rules that will get us in and rules that will kick us out.

BEGINNING OF THE TRADE

We've already discussed some of the methods to enter a trade as well as my personal rules to enter a trade. To sum them up, each trade I take must meet:

1. Fundamental criteria including that which I consider as part of an E.A.G.L.E. stock:
   a. Extraordinary earnings, sales, and/or projections;
   b. Asymmetric reward to risk potential;
   c. Game changer;
   d. Leadership;
   e. Environment.
2. Technical criteria. The stock is set up in an actionable pattern within my system.
3. Score high on the Trade Gauntlet, the weighted average checklist I've developed to make sure I'm taking the best of the best trades. Try it for yourself. Go to tradingmindwheel.com/resources.

If a stock passes all three elements, it's earned a spot in the arena. If it then triggers the entry, it's earned a spot in my portfolio.

It's from here that the management of the trade begins.

Setups

As discussed in the previous chapter, our goal is to enter high-probability trades that offer an asymmetric reward to risk. If we can do this, we can come out way ahead even with a win rate that is seemingly low. Remember, if we flip a coin and get paid $2 on heads and lose $1 on tails, we've got a winning system.

For our system, we should only put money into those setups that have been vetted, proven through the years, and have passed rigorous testing. As 3× US Investing Champion David Ryan has said many times, "There is nothing new under the sun." None of us need to start a system from scratch. We can add to and build upon what already works.

If we don't use what's proven or what's been tested, it is the equivalent of closing our eyes and throwing a dart at the wall. Sure, sometimes we'll hit the target, but that doesn't make it a good idea.

For proven setups that have passed the test of time, review the chapters on analysis.

Slippage

When considering entering any trade, we need to factor in something called "slippage." There are a few ways to think about slippage in a trade, but it basically boils down to these two:

1. The difference between our intended and actual entry price;
2. Transaction fees.

When entering a trade, typically it will be easy to get filled, but it's rare that we'll get in at the exact price we want. This is the first type of slippage. Here's an example.

Suppose we want to buy a stock at $100 even. We place our order, and the price opens above our entry at $101. Do we buy in right there and then? What would you do?

It depends, doesn't it?

How wide was our stop loss? What were we originally planning to risk? If we were planning to risk $5, an extra dollar might be okay. But what if we were planning to risk $2? Our risk just jumped up by 50%!

The tighter our entry, the greater a factor slippage becomes.

But wait, what about short-term swing trading? How about day trading and scalping?

Yes, the more we condense our time frame, the more slippage is a major consideration. A great trade can easily turn into a poor one due to slippage in these cases.

So what do we do in these cases?

Let's start with swing trading.

In swing trading, I like to use what's called a "buy stop limit order." Basically, this allows us to tell our broker the price we'd like the order to trigger at (this is the "buy stop") and once triggered, to buy up to a certain price (this is the limit order).

When placing these types of orders we may wonder how far away to place the limit. Place it too far, and a great trade may become an average trade. Place it too close, and we may not get filled. So what should we do?

My solution is to do the following:

1. If my risk in the trade is greater than or equal to 5%, I'll set my limit order for 1% above the buy stop. In the earlier example, my limit order would have been at $101, and I'd have been filled.

2. If my risk in the trade is less than 5%, I'll divide my risk amount by 5 and then add that amount to buy stop to come up with the limit order. Here's an example:
   a. Entry Signal = $100
   b. Stop Loss = $98
   c. Risk = $100 (entry) − $98 (stop) = $2 (risk)
   d. Limit order = ($2 (risk) / 5 = $0.40) = $100.40 (limit order).

Another way to think of it is to keep our limit order within about ⅕ of our risk. Hopefully, this makes sense. Here's one more example, this time using risk that is greater than 5%.

   a. Entry Signal = $200
   b. Stop Loss = $195
   c. Risk = $200 (entry) − $195 (stop) = $5 (risk)
   d. Limit order = ($5 (risk) / 5 = $1.00) = $201(limit order).

Transaction Fees: Transaction fees have come down dramatically in recent years. Many brokers now offer zero transaction fees. Still, it's worth mentioning here for those of us who trade instruments where transaction fees are still common.

The way to handle transaction fees is to first know the average number of trades we'll take in a year. I say average because we'll likely be above or below this number. That's okay. Like most things in trading, we're not dealing in absolutes.

Suppose we make an average of 200 trades in a year. To keep the math simple, let's say that each trade has just one entry and one exit. We're neither scaling in nor scaling out. In this case, we have 400 transactions per year.

If we're trading options and are being charged $0.50 per contract, that's $200/year in transaction fees.

We can then compare that transaction fee amount to the size of our account.

- On a $10,000, that's 2%;
- On a $100,000, that's 0.2%;
- And so on.

Depending on the size of our account, transaction fees may be quite meaningful or not. If you're starting small as I did (I only started with $5,000, and back then transaction fees were $10/trade—do the math), it can actually work out to be to your advantage when you have acute awareness like this. Knowing that you have a large hurdle to overcome just to break even forces you to focus on the best of the best trades. Don't get me wrong, I'm glad fees have come down and are virtually nonexistent. I'll take that every day of the week. My point is that if you're starting small, you're not as disadvantaged as you may think. Flip the script. View it for what it is. View it positively, and that's what it becomes.

FOUR TYPES OF EXITS

I find it helpful to break exits down into the following categories:

1. Targets;
2. Trails;
3. Back Stops;
4. Stop Losses.

Each of these can be as simple or as complex as we want. The objective here is to give ourselves multiple ways to exit a trade. Just like when we're in a movie theater, there are multiple fire exits, so we should have the same in a trade.

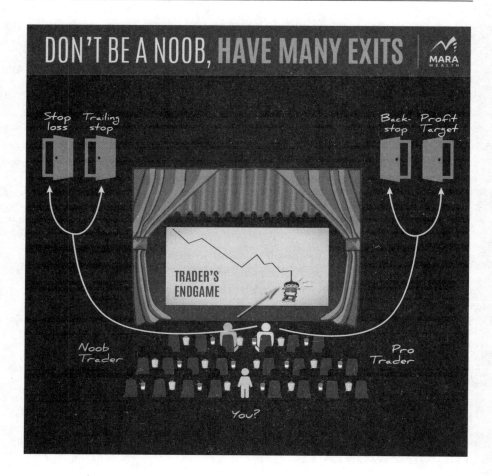

Ideally, we walk into the theater and the movie is as awesome as we expect; think of this as your target price. We have an expectation when we enter the trade, but we don't know how it's going to turn out.

Trailing stops are generally momentum- and time-bound based in one form or another. The simplest kind of trailing stop is based on a percentage. It's overly simplistic and not my preferred kind of stop. It just takes a certain percent off the highest price since we've entered the trade and places a stop below that. Too often this places a stop in an arbitrary place. We can do better. More on that later.

Back stops are used to get out of a trade while the getting is good. For example, if price has been going up and then trades sideways, it develops a new support area. Once it moves higher again, (thereby confirming the support area) if it were to come back and fall through support, we'd exit all or at least a portion of the trade.

Another way to think about it is like walking up a flight of stairs. You get to the top of the stairs, and what was once the ceiling is now the floor. As you walk along the floor you'd know something is wrong if you suddenly fall through it. If god forbid something like that ever were to happen, hopefully, you can catch yourself before falling too far. This is what a back stop does for us.

Finally, the stop loss. This is where we cut our losses short. If we sat down for the movie and 10 minutes in realize that we're in for a snooze fest, we can turn right around and exit from where we came in (unless of course, we want a good nap).

Targets

I like to think of targets as you might think about setting a destination into a GPS. It helps us know if the trade is on track or if it is veering off course. Beyond that, however, targets in trading can be far different. A trade may never reach its "destination," or it may go way past it.

Right about now you might be asking yourself, "But, Mike, why bother setting targets at all if we're not going to hit them or are willing to drive right past them? If you want us to drive east, isn't that good enough to do what you're saying here?"

Great question! Yes, we'd have the general direction, but we'd have no idea about the distance. For example, suppose you came to visit me in Long Island, New York, and we decided to head east. East can bring us down the street and to my favorite coffee house, out to Montauk (the far eastern tip of Long Island) or we can keep going across the Atlantic and head to Europe.

The reason why we want to use a specific target even if we may not hit it is because it helps us gauge the potential of a trade and know right away if it's worth taking.

For example, suppose you want to only take trades that offer a minimum of 3:1 reward to risk. Fairly reasonable, and you can find plenty of those. Now suppose a trade comes along. You do your measurements (including your target), and you find that the trade is offering a 1.5:1 reward to risk. Right away you know to move on. In this way, the target helps us figure out the potential reward-to-risk ratio and can even become part of the selection criteria.

Remember, in trading, we're dealing in the realm of possibilities and probabilities. We're not dealing with absolutes. Given our criteria, we can gauge the potential of a move, and that is plenty good enough.

Trails

In my opinion, trails give us some of the most flexibility and creativity in trading. It's here that through the years I've personally fine-tuned my trading the most, and this is one of the ways I was able to adapt my swing-trading strategy to day trading. It isn't just my results either. This is one of the advanced elements we teach to clients and one that has served so many of our students well. In fact, as I'll share in a moment, one of my former students turned good friend, and now fellow coach Stuart Chalmers, has taken trails to the next level and has come up with an advanced and dynamic approach he refers to as "danger signals."

Starting Out with Trails

When starting out with trails we may have an idea that we're simply raising our stop based on a certain percentage amount below the highest price since we've entered. Suppose we use a 10% trailing stop. If we buy in at $100 and the price jumps to $120, our trailing stop would be at $108 ($120 − 10% = $108).

Sometimes trailing stops in this way work out, and sometimes they don't. My experience has been that they are too hit or miss and too oversimplified. The stop often ends up in no man's land, where there's little or no confluence around that level.

Others may use an ATR (average true range)-based stop. I actually like this one but don't use it straight away as an automatic stop. Rather, I like to use it as one of the danger signals I look for and that we'll discuss shortly. In brief, the ATR looks at the price range over a given period that we select (days, weeks, months, hours, etc.) and a certain lookback period. For my swing trading account, I like to consider a 1.5x 10-period ATR on the daily chart. It looks over the ATR for the past 10 days and multiplies it by 1.5. If the price closes below this, then I take it as one signal that the trend may be shifting against me, and I may want to consider taking action.

Moving averages and aVWAP (anchored volume weighted average price) can be used in a similar way. Each of them moves with price as it progresses.

I'll often hear the question, Which moving average is best?

The truth is that there is no one best moving average. Generally speaking, price has a tendency to trend above or walk along a certain moving average.

When we observe this, it's worth taking note. When that trend starts to change, price is displaying a change in character, and that may serve as a reason to take action. It can really happen on any moving averages on any time frame.

Here are the moving averages I like best and why. I use each of these on a daily chart.

5 ema	Closely follows the short-term trend and shows some of the strongest momentum.
10 ema	The best swing trades often hold the 10 ema.
21 ema	The best intermediate-term trades will hold 21 ema. Many of the best swing trades also start by consolidating along and then bouncing from the 21 ema.
50 sma	This often serves as the line in the sand for intermediate-term traders. Many of the stocks with the biggest moves historically have held their 50 sma for the duration of the trade.
100 ema	Many stocks that slice through their 50 sma in a meaningful way that are not through with their up moves will find support near the 100 ema, the halfway point between the 50 and the 200 sma (not literally but close enough).
200 sma	This is often the line of last resort. Institutions typically step in at this level to defend positions and add more shares. If a stock spends more than a week or two below the 200 sma, it typically indicates more downside is on the horizon.

"Danger Signals" Overview

Danger Signals are an advanced and dynamic approach to trailing stops. Rather than exiting a trade because of any one of the above reasons we've discussed so far, I'll allow them and others to act as "danger signals," a signal that the trade may be finished. The truth is that we never really know when the trend is truly over until after the fact. A moving average or a support level can be breached intra-day just to rebound. A trade can close near its lows for the day or for the week, signaling that at least for that session sellers were in control. But we never know what will happen tomorrow, next week, or next month.

Trading is a game of odds. Therefore, when I find that a trade may be souring, weighing the evidence or danger signals can be extremely helpful.

So how do we do this? *Simple!* The answer is well-crafted checklists that *you* create.

The reason why you must be the creator (even if you're starting with a template like the one we're going to give you) is because being the creator is the only way that it will be representative of your beliefs.

Do you need to begin from scratch? No. We simply need to find examples of what works. From there, we can begin the selection process of what works for us.

I've added my checklist below that you can use as a template. These checklists are working documents. While at the time of this writing, the figures, templates, and thoughts shared are the culmination of over 40 years of living and over 20 years of trading, it's not by any means "done." It's a continuous evolution. Expect that the lists and templates you create for yourself today will evolve in some way six months from now. I personally find that something significant grows about every 90 days. How? It came from the work and the seeds planted in the prior 90 days and continuing that process throughout.

Danger Signals I look For

Here are the Danger Signals I consider as of the time of this writing for swing trades and the points in the trade that I consider them:

- ALL: Price closes near its daily low;
- ALL: Price closes near its weekly low;
- ALL: Price closes near its lows on heavy relative volume;
- ALL: Price closes below its certain moving average;
- ALL: Price closes below short-term swing low;
- ALL: Fast stochastic crosses below slow stochastic;
- ALL: Both fast and slow stochastics are curved down;
- ALL: Price shows aggressive selling (moves higher, closes near lows, on heavy volume);
- ALL: Outside reversal bar that pushes into fresh highs and closes near its lows;
- ALL: Price closes below 1.5 ATR 10 period;
- ALL: Price closes below aVWAP;
- ALL: Price shows signs of "stalling" (heavy volume and little price progress);
- ALL: The market begins to underperform;
- ALL: Price has a character change (e.g. tight and controlled shifting to wide and loose);
- ALL: Three consecutive days of lower lows;
- ALL: Any down day that closes lower than previous three bars;
- OPEN GAME: Tighten up and cut losses quicker if price squats;
- OPEN GAME / END GAME: Price makes a series of lower swing highs and lower swing lows on an intraday chart (30 min.);
- MID GAME / END GAME: Certain moving averages begin crossing below one another;
- MID GAME / END GAME: RS starts curving downward;
- MID GAME / END GAME: RS turns negative short term;
- MID GAME / END GAME: RS underperforms price short term;
- MID GAME / END GAME: Certain moving averages begin to flatten out;
- MID GAME / END GAME: Price shows signs of exhaustion (moves higher on progressively lighter volume);

- MID GAME / END GAME: Price hits a certain % target;
- MID GAME / END GAME: Price hits a certain R multiple target;
- MID GAME / END GAME: Price hits overhead resistance;
- MID GAME / END GAME: Price hits a Fibonacci level;
- MID GAME / END GAME: Price hits a psychological level;
- MID GAME / END GAME: The industry or sector the stock is in begins to underperform;
- MID GAME / END GAME: Price breaks an ascending trend line;
- END GAME: Price structure forms a bearish pattern;
- END GAME: Price shows signs of selling into strength (moves higher, closes near lows);
- END GAME: Certain moving averages begin to slope downward.

Danger Signals Nuances

Signals and our response to them may be different depending on when they occur in the trade.

For example, if we're entering a breakout trade (the style I enjoy) and price bars are closing near their daily highs and on heavy volume, this is a sign that buyers are stepping in aggressively. This type of volume is generated by major institutions with deep pockets. The major institutions can rarely do all of their buying in one shot. It can take them several days or weeks to buy the number of shares they'd like to fill out a position. Therefore, when I see heavy volume buying happening at this stage, I take it as confirmation of the breakout having a higher probability of success.

Now if we were to take that same price bar and instead of at the beginning of the trade, price has already been running for several weeks or even several months without taking much of a breather, the interpretation of that price bar is quite different. Heavy buying at this later stage could be a sign of exhaustion or euphoria. A sign that the entire move may be done and it's time to think about exiting.

How Many Danger Signals Should Trigger an Action?

I think it will depend in part on your objectives as well as the total number of danger signals that you have. For example, my objective is to stay with a trade until it shows signs that momentum is shifting and the trend is about to change. If there are six danger signals or more, that represents a sign, and that sign will trigger some type of action for me, whether that action is to raise a back stop (discussed in the next section), exit a portion of the trade, or exit the entire trade. Presently, six danger signals are the equivalent of 15% of the danger signal checklist.

Here's an example (see Fig 4.4) that happened on August 2, 2022, as I was working on this section of the book. I was long ECPG (I started the position on July 12, 2022, as it was breaking out from a low cheat area). Everything was going great for the majority of the time I was in the trade. Each day, price was showing some sign of accumulation, be it closing high in the daily range, doing so on volume, or if the price was down on the day, closing in the middle of its daily range showing that weakness was being bought. Then all of a sudden on August 2, 2022, ECPG flashed eight danger signals. That was enough of a warning for me to exit the trade entirely.

Two days later, the price fell 14% and counting. This is one example of the power of developing danger signals for yourself. Weighing the evidence, develop rules to help you exit, and take action. See image below.

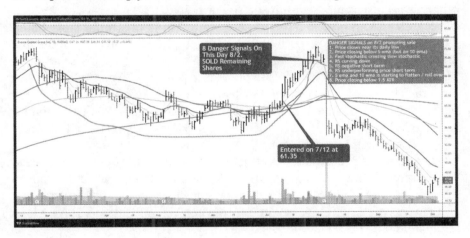

FIG 4.4

To sum up, one of my daughter's vocab words this week is "ACTION," and we needed to put it into a sentence. So timely with this chapter. If you see danger signals developing, take action!

Level 2 Customizing Danger Signals

If you like this concept and are planning to customize it, an effective way to do so is to incorporate your own personal backtesting and results into the equation.

For example, after reviewing his trades, Anthony Iuliano, one of our members, discovered that if the first day he was in a trade it had a "poor close," which he defined as price closing both at the low of the trading range and below the 5 ema, the trade almost always hit his full stop. While this may only hit two of my danger signals, in Anthony's case he may exit the trade fully based on his data.

Other ways to customize danger signals and their use include fine-tuning the number of signals needed during certain market conditions, certain events, or certain types of setups. The list goes on, and you can get really creative here. However, the way to stay on the path and not find yourself caught up in a wild goose chase, chasing your tail, or otherwise stuck in analysis paralysis is to develop your ideas based on the post analysis of your journaling and data collection. This kind of post analysis is what will lead us to our next step of improvement. More on post analysis later.

Back Stops

Back stops offer protection from sudden moves against our position that may otherwise cause us to lose profits or lose principal.

Here's an easy way to think of back stops. Think of a multi-story house or apartment building. You want to get to the third floor. You start on the first floor, walk up the first flight of stairs, and now you're on the second floor. That was pretty easy. You're halfway to where you want to go. And what was once the ceiling to you is now your floor. You walk around the bend to the next flight of stairs. The floor beneath you is pretty sturdy. You trust that it's going to hold up. You approach the next flight of stairs and start climbing.

That second floor can now be thought of as your back stop.

Let's say you're carrying something up the stairs and you drop it. Instead of dropping all the way back to the first floor where you started, it drops to the second floor. You go back down a few steps, pick it up, and continue on.

This is what back stops can do for us when we're in a trade. Have a look at the following price chart (see Fig 4.5).

FIG 4.5

This stock (ticker PRVA) is a stock that Anthony brought up in discussion today, August 2, 2022. Do you see how price steadily moved up over time? Do you see how price formed a set of boxes, almost like a set of stairs, and then continued its accent?

In this way, price has built its own "ceiling" and its own "floor." When price falls through the floor (eventually it will), we can use that as our cue to sell part or all of the trade. And when price moves like this, we can tell where the floor is and what floor we're on.

One more thing to mention before we move on is when we're thinking about back stops and we're considering how sturdy of a floor they may have developed, look for confluences around the bottom of the "floor levels."

Using the same example in PRVA, do you notice the moving average line below the price bars? That happens to be the 21 ema (21-period exponential moving average). It is now providing a layer of support to the floor. So if the floor level is breached (the bottom of the box), it will have also taken out the 21 ema and will likely have posted a number of the danger signals we mentioned earlier.

This is what we're talking about when we talk about confluences.

Stop Loss

The stop loss is the exit that helps us keep our losses small. Losses work exponentially against us. If we're not careful, losses can put us in a hole that is difficult to climb out of. Stop losses help prevent the hole from getting too deep.

To go back to the movie analogy from earlier, think of a stop loss as the doors in the back of the theater (the ones we entered through). If we need to leave before the movie is through (fire, bathroom break, or if the movie is a snooze fest), we can walk right out the back door.

Stop losses should be preplanned. We should know where we will exit with a loss before the trade ever gets executed. This makes it far easier to act in the moment when the time is necessary. I personally prefer to place a stop loss order with my broker that is "GTC" (good till canceled).

The way it works is that once price crosses the level I've set, a market order is automatically generated, and I get filled at whatever the market price happens to be at the time. This is why we want to be mindful of where we place our stop loss.

Similar to back stops, the ideal spot will have several layers of confluence. Use what is a part of your system. If you don't have a system or are considering adding to your system, here are the confluences I look for when setting a stop:

- A stop below a short-term swing low on a daily chart;
- Price is the swing low on a weekly chart;

- The distance between the stop and my entry point is about 5% (5% is the average; sometimes it can be as much as 10% or as little as 2% on a swing trade, but most of the time, it ends up being close to 5%);
- A moving average is near the swing low (my preference is for the 21 ema or 50 sma; for extremely high momentum trades the 10 ema or 5 ema is okay);
- Fibonacci retracement levels;
- Trend lines;
- aVWAP.

Whether you're using these elements or something else, the more you find that are lining up, the better. I'll also often place my stop below the closest round number. Suppose support happens to be 95.15, I'll place my stop at 94.90

WHEN TO SELL IN STAGES VS. WHEN TO SELL IT ALL

There will be times in our trading when the proper move will be to sell bits and pieces. There will be other times when it will be appropriate to exit the entire trade (as in the case of the example with ECPG mentioned earlier).

How do we know which is which?

This question can lead to a lot of confusion, and it trips up novice and intermediate traders alike. The reason lies in the question itself. If we're attempting to intellectualize the answer, we're acting as the player, not the game master. If we're acting as the game master, then the way we know if we should exit in full or partially is by looking at the rules of our game. If our rules are unclear, we know what to focus on, adding clarity.

Here's how I've gone about making sell decisions on my swing trades and why.

- Sell half at average win: My average win is about 10%. I want to be out of half the trade when I get to this level. If the trade sours at this point, then at least I've locked in half at my average win. If the trade continues higher from this point, then at least I've held onto half my trade for the bigger move (selling half in this way is a tactic I learned from Mark Minervini).

- Sell all when stop loss is hit: Our stop loss should be preplanned. I prefer to use hard stops and place them with my broker. The moment price is crossed, I'm out.
- Sell partials into strength: When I've made multiples beyond my average win, I'll exit partials into strength. The partial amounts can be anywhere from as little as 5% of what I have left to as much as half. Here it depends on a combination of market conditions, the behavior of the trade, and personal performance. These gray zones highlight spots where I can fine-tune and evolve.
- Sell partials on weakness: Selling on weakness occurs in three ways:
  1. Stop Loss;
  2. Back Stops;
  3. Trails.

    Stop losses and back stops give us the opportunity to preplan precisely where we'll exit and how much. Most commonly the exits are in full, but they don't have to be. We can exit partially using what Mark Minervini calls a "split stop."

    Suppose we're in a trade like PRVA, mentioned earlier, and it's working out well. We'd like to raise our stop to protect our gains but are concerned about choking off the trade. A solution is to use a "split stop" where part of our stop is at one level, and part is at another level. Personally, I find that splitting the number of shares evenly between the two is the best way to go about doing it. It's the only way that hasn't left me feeling regret to either have sold more if price fell further or to have sold less if price continued on.

- Sell all into strength: When price has a parabolic move, it's time to sell into strength. No one wants to be the bag holder. Selling everything into strength can feel very counterintuitive. Not only has the trade done exactly what we had hoped for when we sold into strength, but price can also often continue to move higher. Thus we can end up feeling like a stooge for having sold too early.

Successful trading is not about the gains we once had. Nor is it about the gains we could have had. It's about the gains we actually keep.

If for example price has a gigantic move similar to GME, AMC, or TLRY, (see Fig 4.6–4.9) we need to start selling into strength, and sell everything, because price is flashing signs of euphoria. Everyone thinks the asset is going to the moon and are buying in droves. Price is skyrocketing and so is volume. The question then becomes, if everyone is buying, who will be left to continue driving up the price?

Bag holders find out the hard way that the answer is no one. In a flash, all the demand came rushing in. Demand dwarfed supply, which sent the price skyrocketing. Eventually, demand exhausts itself, and there are no more buyers. Now there's no place for price to go but down. And that is why we want to sell on the way up. It's far better to sell into strength when there's loads of demand and it's easy to unload shares. On the way down, seemingly everyone is trying to sell. Demand dries up, and massive selling takes over. The bid and the ask spreads can often be very wide. Price can have major gap downs. You may have trouble getting your order filled. **This is what is meant when people say they would "rather be out of a trade wishing they were in than to be in a trade and wishing they were out!"**

Sometimes we hear about trades that are life-changing. There can be many of those for each of us in the market. However, if we want to experience the ones that are life-changing for the better, we had best sell into strength on moves like these while the getting is good and not end up as one of the bag holders. Even if we later find out that we sold way too early and price runs another 500% without us, it's better than watching our gains get cut in half or worse turn into losses.

Here's the chart of TLRY (see Fig 4.6). An epic move of +900% in only 24 trading days! I recall one of my Instagram followers, Alex, reaching out to me on September 19, 2018, as TLRY was approaching $250/share asking for advice. He was already up 500% and was considering adding.

"This is one of the biggest parabolic moves I've personally witnessed," I told Alex. "First off, congrats on being in this trade to begin with. Second, this is not the time to add. It's the time to sell and to sell it all!"

"But the cannabis market is just getting started, Mike! I think Tilray is one of the leaders."

"It may very well be one of the leaders, Alex. It may end up becoming the leader of the entire industry. However, what we're talking about right now is the stock, not the company. When any stock moves like this, it's only moments away from topping out. Maybe it can come back, but the odds are stacked against it. And let's say it does come back. Wouldn't it be better to sell now, lock in the gains, and buy back at half the price or less?"

"I hadn't thought about it that way . . . thanks, Mike!"

Alex sold at about $270. Price ultimately topped out at $300 before closing at $214.06 on the day. The following day the price dropped to $176.35. At the time of this writing, TLRY is trading at $3.89.

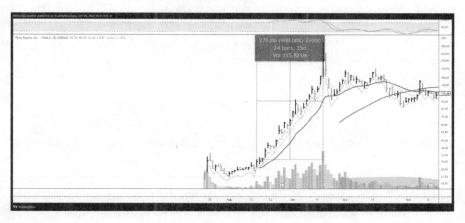

FIG 4.6

Sometimes lightning can strike twice, and in the case of AMC, it did!

AMC had two parabolic moves within about six months of each other. The first ran +922% in 15 trading days (see Fig 4.7) ultimately topping out on January 27, 2021. The second ran +582% in 13 trading days (see Fig 4.8) ultimately topping out on June 2, 2021. This is a great example of why we should continue to keep trades on the radar even if we missed them. Once a trade gives us the signal and has proven worthy of entering the arena, it's our job to allow it onto the field.

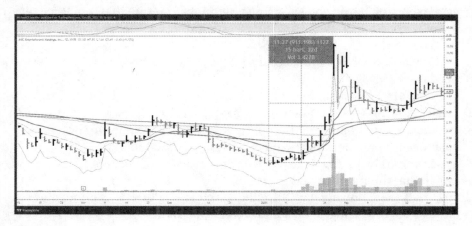

FIG 4.7

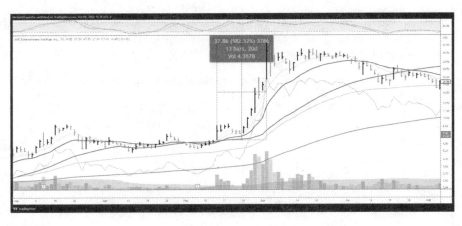

FIG 4.8

Next is GME. In only 95 trading days it ran a staggering +8,128%. When price ultimately topped on January 28, 2021, at $120.75 the biggest trending conversation globally on Twitter was, "Hold the line." Catastrophic losses were just around the corner. Not weeks, not days, but hours away. Price closed −60% off its peak, finishing the day at $48.40.

The market has an incredible way to dish out lessons to those who need them. We can receive those lessons the easy way through other people's experiences and in books like this, or we can get them the hard way.

Many people opted for the hard way with GME.

The next day on January 29, 2021, the price opened at $94.93. Being a holder was vindicated. Those who held on breathed a sigh of relief. Many of them were ready to double down on their holdings. Many of them did. There were plenty of "I told you so" going around the Internet that day. Price ultimately closed the day at $81.25, up an astounding 67.97% on the day.

The wins would be short-lived.

The following day, on February 1, 2021, price dropped to $56.25, closing the day 30% lower.

The rally cries came even louder on Twitter and throughout the Internet. "Hold the line" was trending once again, and this time with even more conviction. And why not? Holding on, adding to, and even starting new positions in GME had all worked two days ago, didn't it?

Everyone who had held, added, or started new positions had a rude awakening the following day. GME opened the day at $35.19, down about 30% from the following day. Price didn't rebound either. It continued to sell off, and sell off—and sell off some more.

GME finished February 2, 2021, down an astounding 60%, finishing the day with a closing price of only $22.50.

Outcries of manipulation, the "1% are against us," "Down with Robin Hood," and "This is all their fault" were rampant. Fingers were being pointed everywhere except for the one place that could actually make a difference in their accounts, that could do something to improve their performance. I think you know who I'm talking about.

See the chart of GME below (Fig 4.9).

FIG 4.9

The more responsibility we're willing to take, the more control we have. When we give away responsibilities by pointing the finger, we also give away our power to change, our power to improve, our power to do anything.

The market gives us an incredible opportunity. But that opportunity is only available to us when we accept full responsibility, not play the victim.

WHEN TO ADD

There is really only one time to add to a position, and it's when our setup appears. If you don't have a setup, get one. Review the chapter on Analysis for help.

Whenever we enter the market, whether we are starting a brand-new position or adding to an existing one, we always want it to be a high-probability, high-reward to low-risk trade. Period.

Now we may have multiple types of setups in our repertoire. We may choose to wait for a fresh base pattern. We may have special "add-on" setups (we'll discuss these in a moment). We may add when we are at a profit. There are even some circumstances where we might add even if we're at a loss! I know, blasphemy, right? We'll discuss that as well. In fact, let's discuss it right now.

Adding to a Losing Trade (Advanced and Not for the Faint of Heart)

Adding to a position when we're sitting at a loss is definitely an advanced tactic. It's not for the faint of heart. In fact, it's not necessary to do at all if your goal is simply to achieve consistent, profitable growth. I'm even a little hesitant to include this tactic in this book. However, one of my goals with this book is to share with you everything that has worked for me, everything that has worked for my clients, and to share with you the nuts, bolts, and mindsets that go along with it. So here we go.

As a trade approaches our planned stop loss, something miraculous happens to our risk-reward ratio. It expands geometrically!

Let's think about it like this. If you bought a stock at $100 and set a stop at $95, how much are you risking per share? $5, right?

Now suppose the price drops and is now $96. Your stop is at $95. How much risk is there now?

How you view this question says a lot about how you view risk and reward. You may be thinking there is still $5 but is there really? Price is already at $96, and at this point you've already lost $4. You may not have exited the trade, but that $4 is already gone. That's okay. It's how you set up the trade to begin with, *AND* it may come back. You'd allow the price to drop to $95 before exiting with a loss. So if the price drops to $96, there is really only $1 left.

If our stop is placed well with lots of confluence around it, it serves as an excellent line in the sand. Anything below it, and we're no longer interested in the trade, right? (At least at this stage.)

So as price gets closer and closer to our stop, the reward side of the ratio becomes even more heavily skewed in our favor.

Let's say our target is $120 and we entered at $100 and our stop is $95. This is a 4:1 reward-to-risk trade, right?

If price drops to $96, we've already said that there is $1 of risk left in the trade. So if there is $1 of risk left and our target is still $120, how much reward is there now? $24, right? So our 4:1 reward to risk just jumped to 24:1.

Take a moment to allow this to sink in.

Now before you run off and attempt this, what roles do you think probability and position sizing play? If you said, "Quite a bit," then you're absolutely right. This is one of the ways many of the spokes of the mind wheel come together and the market really can turn into an infinite stream of opportunity.

I've seen trades come within as little as $0.02 of hitting my stop loss. If our stops are well placed, they should hold. If they get tripped, it's a sign something is wrong and we should exit.

So let's continue with our example above, and let's assume we have a $1 million account to help us keep the math nice and simple.

Suppose we want to allocate 20% of our capital to this trade. That'd be $200,000.

Let's also say that we'd like to risk no more than 1% of our capital ($10,000) on this trade.

So if we enter at $100 with a stop of $95, we'd be able to buy 2,000 shares.

Now suppose price does drop to $96. We analyze the stock and the market, and determine that it's finding support and that there is a 50/50 shot at a bounce. We decide that we want to add to our position because we now have a 24:1 reward to risk and 50/50 odds. How much should we add?

To answer this question, we need to think about our worst-case scenario. Unless you're a day trader, you're going to have overnight risk. And if you're trading stocks, this means that price may gap against you. This must be factored into how many shares you'll add if you're going to attempt this at all.

Suppose for example that you determine the next level of major support is at $85. If you decide you're willing to take another $1,000 of risk (remember, we're working off a $1 million account, so $1,000 is only 0.1% of capital), you'll be able to buy about 90 shares.

Here's the fun part, let's assume that the worst-case scenario doesn't play out *BUT* you do get stopped out of the trade at $95. You've only lost an additional $90! Your upside on this (assuming price runs to the $120 target) is $2,160!

Remember, our goal is to find high-probability asymmetrical reward-to-risk trades. The math has to work in our favor to attempt this. In this example, we said that we had 50/50 odds of a bounce. We also said that our absolute worst case was a drop to $85 (what would end up being a $990 loss on this add-on). Basically what we've found here was another coin flip scenario where we get paid $2 if we win, and lose $1 if we lose. I'll take those kinds of trades all day.

What we need to avoid, however, is the deal where the odds are terrible. For example, if we were getting a 24:1 reward to risk but the odds of winning were 1 out of 100, it'd be a losing game. Similar to the lottery or just about any game in Vegas. Remember, in trading, we want to operate like the casino, not the gamblers. We are the game masters, and we're putting the odds in our favor.

Adding to a Winning Trade

Adding to a winning trade is a bit easier. We already have confirmation that our trade is a winner. The question becomes should we add to it? If so, when?

What we want to do is define certain traits that when met tell us that it's a time to add. Just as we discussed earlier, we always want the reward-to-risk ratio, as well as the odds, to be heavily skewed in our favor. It's our job to determine when those times occur.

Here are some of the things I consider and some that you may want to consider too:

1. Have you already achieved your average gain on the trade?
2. How far has the trade moved already? Is it late in its run?
3. How far is the trade from major support levels?
4. Are there any major events coming up soon that you should be aware of, such as earnings announcements or a new product launch?
5. How long has price consolidated?

Generally, I prefer for price to consolidate for at least two weeks, typically longer, before I consider adding. I'll look for the price patterns discussed in the analysis chapter plus the following:

- Flags;
- Pennants;
- Triangles.

Each of these patterns tends to form when a stock is already in an uptrend, has broken out, and is pausing briefly before resuming its uptrend.

Here we need to consider the amount that price has already run. The further price has run, the later it is in its move and the more likely sellers are to drive the price back down. It is for this reason that we'll want to consider buying less on an add-on than what we purchased initially.

Here's another way to think about it.

Suppose you bought at $100. Price runs to $120 and then forms a pennant. Price bounces between $120 and $115. Eventually, it drops a bit more, and gives a new entry point at $118 with support at $115. You can add to this trade here while risking $3/share.

The idea is to add to a winning trade. The winning trade isn't the profits in our account per se. The winning trade is the player in the game that is performing well. Just like a pitcher that may have been scheduled to pitch for seven innings, but to this point has pitched a no-hitter. The coach decides to send him out for the eighth and ninth innings. He's been pitching a while now, has used up some energy, and the other team has experienced his pitching, so the odds of someone getting a hit are higher than they were at the start of the game. These are the same factors to consider when adding to a trade. How much? Two innings for the pitcher, perhaps a third of the original trading position for us traders depending on how far along the trade is, where major support is, and all the other factors mentioned above.

Sometimes the add-on will be as clear as day and a no-brainer. Other times it may be a close call. The way I draw a line in the sand is to run every trade setup through the Trade Gauntlet. We talked about the Trade Gauntlet earlier, so I won't go into detail about it here. As a reminder though, you can use the Trade Gauntlet for free. Go to tradingmindwheel .com/resources.

DEALING WITH EARNINGS ANNOUNCEMENTS

Volumes have been written on trade management. If you'd like to go deeper, I encourage you to continue your research. The final point I'd like to make here involves earnings announcement.

I don't know about you, but I've often heard people say that earnings is a "crap shoot" and to just stay away from it. I'm a big fan of doing what works and what serves you best, so if this is it, by all means, stick with it. However, what I've found more often is that the "stay away from earnings announcements because they're a crap shoot" is simply fear taking over the decision-making process. Personally, I think we can do better than this.

When we consider earnings announcements or really any kind of major event (product announcement, a takeover, news from the Fed, wars, etc.), the effect on the market is increased odds of volatility, and we don't know if that volatility will work for us or against us. In the stock market, prices can gap in either direction.

What this basically means to us is that the reward-to-risk ratio changes.

So the question to ask ourselves is, How can we best manage the reward-to-risk ratio?

There are a number of ways we can do this both from the onset as well as mid-trade. Some of this may sound familiar to you:

1. Gauge distance to major support: If I'm in the middle of a trade and earnings is tomorrow, I know that it's a potentially high-volatility event. I want to know what my odds of the trade continuing are

(counting up danger signals helps us with this) as well as what my new reward to risk on the trade from its current point is.

   a. If the trade is extended from major support as it was in the case of ECPG mentioned earlier, what was a 4:1 trade may all of a sudden turn into a 1:1 or less at that particular stage. This factor cannot be ignored. It's why so many people refuse to hold through earnings. However, if you're someone who wants to hold for the bigger move, you'll need to hold through earnings sometimes. I'm a swing trader, and I'll still hold through earnings if the odds and the reward to risk are in my favor. Is the game set up to win? This is the question to ask ourselves.

2. Determine the mode by which you'll play.

   a. If buying stock, have a look at the worst-case scenario similar to the above. Take the trade but size as if the worst case were going to happen. If it does, you'll be out the dollar amount you had planned for. If price stops you out at the normal stop, you'll lose significantly less.

   b. Using options to mitigate risk. A tactic that can work quite well is buying options. Entire books have been dedicated to the subject, so we won't go into great detail here. However, the specific tactic I'll sometimes use when buying ahead of earnings is to:

      i. See if the stock has options contracts available;

      ii. If it does, determine whether this particular options market is liquid;

      iii. If it is liquid and I'm going long, buying contracts about 4–6 weeks out with a strike price that is at the breakout price;

      iv. Consider the premium to be the risk in the trade and size accordingly.

This creates a low-risk, high-reward trade that fits well within my system for a few reasons:

1. If the trade works, I'll be at a profit immediately, having bought ahead of earnings.

2. If the trade fails, the most I could lose is my full premium. Since I'm buying contracts with 4–6 weeks until expiration, it's unlikely that I'll lose my full premium. I'll still have some time value.

The catch is that there are relatively fewer of these trades available because we need all four parts mentioned to be present in addition to all of the other requirements for our setup.

PORTFOLIO MANAGEMENT: The BIG Picture and Assessing Our Total Risk

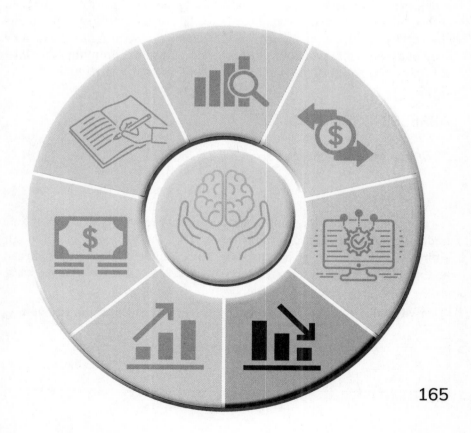

This is a relatively small chapter, but it takes much of what we've learned so far and adds a fresh perspective. Many things in life are like this, aren't they? We can see the finite "things" the world has to offer, but the ways in which we can look at these things are infinite. It is in this way that we gain an ever growing, ever deeper understanding and appreciation of these things.

Assessing your total risk is the second-to-last chapter but a crucial spoke on the trading mindwheel to lead you full circle on this journey. We've spoken quite a bit about our risk in an individual trade. But what about the total risk in our portfolio? How about if we're carrying multiple portfolios? What's our risk then? Do we have what I call a "sh*t hits the fan plan"?

Perhaps this sounds a bit crude, but we must have a plan for when things go absolutely haywire. Thinking about our worst-case scenarios may not seem like a lot of fun. If you're a positivity person like me, it may feel uncomfortable. But putting these plans in place is what helps us build the foundational confidence to take the bigger risks as we move up the ladder.

I once heard that a good engineer can tell you the maximum height a building is going to be just by looking at the hole in the ground. That hole provides the foundation for which the building can stand sturdy, tall, and can withstand the elements. We want our financial portfolios to stand tall. In this chapter, we're taking on the role of that engineer. We're figuring out how deep our hole is and what our portfolios can withstand. From there we'll be able to put measures in place to prevent disasters from occurring.

ASSESSING "PORTFOLIO HEAT"

If you can't stand the heat, get out of the kitchen!

—President Harry Truman

It's one thing to figure out how much risk we're willing to accept in one trade. It's another to figure out how much risk we're willing to accept in our entire portfolio. The two go hand in hand but are different. The same math can be applied. I've added the chart down below to save you from referencing back.

Drawdown % in Trading Capital	Return % to Get Back to Even
−5%	5.3%
−10%	11.1%
−15%	17.6%

Drawdown % in Trading Capital	Return % to Get Back to Even
−20%	25.0%
−25%	33.3%
−30%	42.9%
−35%	53.8%
−40%	66.7%
−45%	81.8%
−50%	100.0%
−55%	122.2%
−60%	150.0%
−65%	185.7%
−70%	233.3%
−75%	300.0%
−80%	400.0%
−85%	566.7%
−90%	900.0%
−95%	1900.0%

So how much risk should we accept? To get the answer, apply the math from earlier. The larger the loss in our portfolio, the more difficult it is to get back to even. Use this chart to begin to calculate how much of a total drawdown your system is able to handle. Remember, we're talking about systems. If you're a thrill seeker, that's great. More power to you. But if your trading system is only able to handle a 5% drawdown before going bust, you better play to that.

Here's a different example. Suppose your system's average gain on each trade is in the neighborhood of 17.6% and its win rate is about 50%; then, if your drawdown begins to exceed 15%, you're headed for trouble.

So what do we do? How can we better manage this?

Perhaps you've heard that the exchanges have "circuit breakers" set up that will halt trading. They are in place to help prevent catastrophes from happening. You can do something similar and prevent catastrophes from happening to your trading account.

Circuit breakers would have helped Paul, a trader who came to me for advice after a devastating near-round trip of Bitcoin.

PAUL'S STORY

Paul started out with about $100,000 in his account. He went all in on Bitcoin in April 2017. He rode it up and saw his account balloon to a whopping $1,467,000 in just eight months! When he finally sold his Bitcoin in November of 2018, however, he walked away with $269,000. Still up 169% on the trade, but when you were once up 1,367% . . .

"WTF?!" Paul exclaimed. Part anger. Part frustration. Part sadness.

It took Paul a while to fully comprehend what happened. In reality, he had made several mistakes and was lucky to be walking away with anything, let alone over a quarter of a mil.

Paul made several mistakes. Are you able to name some of the mistakes Paul made given what you've learned in this book so far? Grab a pen and some paper and list them out.

The first mistake Paul made was going in without an exit strategy. A bad idea when you're using only a portion of your account, let alone all of it. This mistake could have caused Paul's account to be completely annihilated. He got lucky. Had this trade gone the other way, that would have been it.

The next big mistake Paul made was that he had no game plan on how to take profits. Even if he had used just one of the selling strategies from the previous chapter, Paul would have locked in a small fortune. The combination of not having a plan and having tied his ego to being "right" on his analysis resulted in over a million dollars in profit slipping through his fingers.

Paul was used to being right in his analysis. In fact, it's what led to his success in business. Paul owned his own shipping business and relied on his knack for timing the prices of imports and exports to survive and thrive. He concluded that his success at timing imports and exports would translate into timing the market and would do the same with Bitcoin.

Within a few weeks, Paul had been proven right, or so he thought. His account had already more than doubled, and in his mind, that was all the proof he needed. Why bother with an exit strategy? His analysis got him in, and his analysis would get him out, or so he thought.

Bitcoin did have a few pullbacks and consolidations during its run. But each time it pulled back, it snapped right back up. In fact, one week in November 2017, Bitcoin was down over 20%, and the next week it jumped 38%!

Sometimes when trades go to the moon, our heads can get stuck in the clouds. This is what happened to Paul. This is especially true when we don't have rules, any kind of a written trading plan, or a selling strategy.

Paul had survived some wicked pullbacks in Bitcoin before. When it dropped over 40% the week of December 18, 2017, it had not occurred to him that perhaps it would be a good idea to exit at least some of the position. No, Paul dug in his heels and continued to hold.

"I'm right, it's going back up," Paul told himself.

Down $200,000.

"I know I'm right. It's going back up," Paul reaffirmed.

Down $500,000.

"Well, it can't go any lower, this thing is going to bounce."

And finally, in November 2018, the pain got to be too much, and Paul sold. Still walking away with $269,000. But when you had $1,467,000, walking away with $269k feels like a big loss. (See Fig 5.2.)

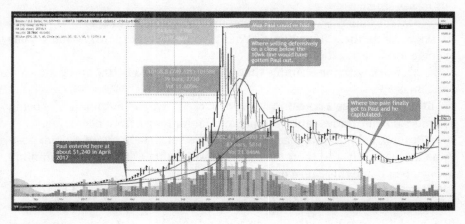

FIG 5.2

People would rather be right more than they want to make money.

—Ed Seykota

There are a number of things Paul could have done differently, aren't there? Even a simple rule of selling anytime Bitcoin dropped more than 50% would have enabled him to walk away with another half mil in his pocket.

Perhaps the most important thing Paul needs to change is his mindset, starting with his definition of what it means to be "right." What if Paul's definition of being right changed to flawlessly executing a time-tested trading strategy? What if Paul flipped his mindset from being a player to being a game master as we spoke of previously?

SETTING UP CIRCUIT BREAKERS

First, let's think back to our chapters on risk management. Recall the idea of "progressive exposure." Progressive exposure works in part because markets and stocks trend. As we begin to see winning ideas emerge and confirm, we can begin scaling up. This allows our prior wins to finance the additional risk we're taking in the larger size. This gives us the opportunity to win *big* if the trend continues and to only go back to even if it doesn't. Applying the same concept on the way down, continuously reducing our trade size as the market moves against us and is no longer confirming that the trend is intact, keeps our losses small.

Now let's take this concept and set up our circuit breakers.

Start with these questions: What's your average gain? What's your average loss?

Let's work with the example that your average gain is 10% and your average loss is 5%.

If we experience a portfolio drawdown of 5%, we can automatically begin scaling back our trades rapidly to prevent larger losses from occurring.

"But what about 'snap back rallies'? If we get shaken out of several positions momentarily and then the market resumes its trend higher? Wouldn't using a tactic like this cause us to miss out?"

It wouldn't necessarily cause us to miss out per se. We would be trading smaller, and so our upside might not be quite as large. However, our objective is to stay in sync with the market and to take a risk-first approach. If market conditions become less favorable, scaling down is the proper answer. Sure, we may occasionally miss out on some larger upswings. However, if our analysis shows that the odds are against us, we should reduce our size. We don't know the future, and those trades could have easily gone the other way. Focus on high-probability, high-reward to low-risk trades.

Streaks occur frequently in the market, and they occur in all trading systems. As mentioned earlier in the analysis chapters, we can actually use these streaks as part of our interpretation of the market. Here's a simple chart that Stuart Chalmers developed for us in-house displaying the losing streaks you can expect given a certain win rate.

| Win Rate | Probable Losing Streaks | | | | |
| | Number of Trades | | | | |
	10	20	50	100	200
30	6	8	11	13	15
32	6	8	10	12	14
34	6	7	9	11	13
36	5	7	9	10	12
38	5	6	8	10	11
40	5	6	8	9	10
42	4	5	7	8	10
44	4	5	7	8	9
46	4	5	6	7	9
48	4	5	6	7	8
50	3	4	6	7	8
55	3	4	5	6	7
65	2	3	4	4	5
80	1	2	2	3	3
90	1	1	2	2	2

Note: Based on pure math and assuming perfect execution of same criteria.
Table shows max expected losing streak by number of trades.
Formula: $LN(n)/-LN(1 - SR/100))$; n=number trades; SR = win rate.

Using myself as an example, my win rate fluctuates between 40% and 50%, and I actually take close to 200 trades per year on average. This means that in any given year, I can expect a losing streak of 8 or even 10 losses in a row. That may seem tough to swallow, but this is why a combination of those mindset exercises we spoke about, position sizing, and now setting up circuit breakers are so important. These mechanisms enable me to keep my ego in check so that if I get five losses in a row (and I lose 5%), I know that scaling down immediately is the right answer because the math works out.

Suppose we're at loss number 5, and this is the start of one of those 10 trade-losing streaks. If we cut our position size in half and rack up five more losers, instead of being down 10%, we now have a 7.5% drawdown. This is still within the "easy to recover" range from the table provided earlier.

To summarize, calculate your win rate, the size of your average gain, and the size of your average loss. Also, consider the average number of trades you'll take in a year. Using those numbers, plug them into the tables and the calculations we discussed earlier. Find the breaking point of your system. For EAGLE (my stock swing trading system), once I hit a 5% drawdown, it's time to start scaling things down to keep myself safe.

Know that the results assume that you're executing your system flawlessly. Even with 25 years of experience I still operate at about a 97% efficiency level. There's always room for improvement. We must keep striving.

And if you're just starting out, plug in the numbers (average gain, loss, etc.) of the system you're starting out with, whether it's mine or someone else's. This will give you a baseline. Once you begin you'll want to track your stats and then plug in your own numbers.

Hopefully, this makes enough sense to give you a solid start. We could go significantly deeper, but this would then become a book unto its own. For now, I'll let you do the math, and if you have questions, please reach out to me via tradingmindwheel.com/resources. I want to help.

POST ANALYSIS:
Step Two of Continuous Improvement

The first six skills that we've discussed up to this point will get you far. What we're about to discuss right now is a large part of what will keep you going. Done well, post analysis can help us discover the themes between what's working well for you and what isn't. It can help you course-correct and better plan the road ahead.

One of the reasons we discussed journaling in such depth is because our post analysis can only be as good as our journaling. Think about it. If the data we have is inconsistent, poorly organized, or overly generalized, how do you think our post analysis will go? Not so good!

Once we've gathered our data, we want to begin analyzing. Ground-breaking stuff, I know. But you'd be surprised at how few people journal and how many fewer people actually put their journaling to use through post-trade analysis. It is mind-boggling how much is being left on the table when we don't post analyze. Don't let this be you.

WHAT TO INCLUDE IN POST ANALYSIS? HOW LONG AND HOW OFTEN?

I'll give you a template to develop a baseline of what to include in your post analysis. It will ultimately be up to you how much or how little you want to do. Know, however, that what you put in is what you'll get out. If you do the bare minimum, that's exactly what you'll get. Most people take a quick peak at their year at the end of the year, swear that the following year will be "their year," come up with a set of New Year's resolutions, and that's it. How do you think that typically works out? Most people aren't growing as much as they could, nor are they maximizing their potential, and this is one of the biggest reasons why. They are not checking their progress, only checking a box on their to-do list.

So what can we do to ensure our progress?

Step 1: Break out the calendar.

Step 2: Schedule weekly post-analysis sessions for yourself. This is where you will spend time reviewing the entire week. Start by blocking off an hour for this task. You may find that some weeks you need a little more time, others you might need less. Find what works for you. If you can, try to find a consistent day and time for this activity. Make it a priority. If it must happen, it will happen. If you say you'll try to do it, that leaves too much wiggle room to slough it off, and then you'll be right back where you started. Don't let that happen. Commit and stick to it.

Step 3: Schedule monthly post-analysis sessions. This is where you review the month. Give yourself a few hours for this task. If it seems too daunting to block off a few hours, you can break it up. If you find it difficult to block out this time, ask yourself why. What's getting in the way? Review your goals and the reasons why trading is so important to you. Post analysis plays an important part in achieving them. For a period of time, my post analysis was done partially during my lunch hour, and partially on my train ride home from work.

Step 4: Quarterly review. For this, you'll likely need half a day. If your goals and trading are important enough to you, surely you can find half a day four times a year.

Step 5: Half-year review. This may take you a full day.

Step 6 Full-year review. This may take you 1–2 days.

Get all of your time blocked on the calendar. When it is on the calendar, it is far more likely to happen. Should something come up, you'll be able to reschedule that much better.

What to Include?

Great post analysis comes down to asking and answering questions. If we want to improve our post analysis, we must improve the quality of the questions we ask ourselves. Weak, disempowering, or overly generalized questions won't work.

Want to improve? We need to do better than asking, "How can I improve?" Our brains operate best when we give them something specific to focus on.

"What were the common traits among my top 10 biggest winners last year?" Now that's a great question! If you answered this question, do you think it would lead you toward a very specific way for you to improve? Absolutely!

If you had a bad month, quarter, or year, don't ask, "How can I stop losing money?" Not only is this question overly generalized, but it's also very disempowering. There are lots of ways to stop losing money. Ask yourself a question like this especially when you're in a negative state and see what kinds of answers come back to you. I'll save you the trouble of going through this—they won't be good.

Here's a better question to ask: "What were the common traits among my top 10 biggest losing trades last year?" Would this lead you to a better solution? You bet! You'd have something concrete to focus on that you could stop doing that would yield immediate results.

Do you see a trend developing here? This is one of the reasons why it's so important to track our trades. If we have only the raw data in place (entries, exits, and position size, for example), we'd have a great start. But if we go a step further in our journaling (see journaling chapters) and write out our reasons for taking the trades, what we liked, what we didn't like, market conditions, any thoughts popping into our heads about the trade throughout the day, the management of the trade, and so forth, we'll be able to go back in time and question beliefs with some real firepower. As you may already know, some beliefs may be very difficult to let go of. I can tell you this is true from firsthand experience. However, when we have real evidence, real experience, and a great question that leads to an open mind, it makes pulling those mental weeds a *LOT* easier. Plus it gives us something much better to plant in its place.

This is precisely how we develop an ever-growing, ever-improving, mental garden. This process can obviously be used in trading. It can also be applied to other parts of life. Try it, and let me know the results. Just tag me on any of my social media.

GETTING ORGANIZED

We want to post analyze with the intention to improve. To do this, we'll need to get organized. We can do this easily by batching our trades. This is where using spreadsheets can really come in handy. Run a pivot table, and you have this info almost instantly. Don't know how to run a pivot table? Trust me, it isn't hard. If you have any experience at all with spreadsheets, give me 15 minutes, and I'll have you up and running with it. The cool part is that you don't even have to spend money on software. You can use Google Sheets for free (at least you can as of the time of this writing) in the same way as you would use MS Excel.

Here are a few ways you might batch your trades:

- Winning trades, losing trades, trades that we saw but didn't take;
- Biggest winning trades;
- Biggest losing trades.

From here we can drill down deeper into specific subsets:

- Market conditions of the biggest winning trades;
- Market conditions for the biggest losing trades;
- Types of setups for the biggest winning trades;
- Types of setups for the biggest losing trades;
- Quality of biggest winning trades (however you grade your trades);
- Quality of biggest losing trades (however you grade your trades);
- Other qualities of your biggest winner;
- Other qualities of your biggest loser;
- Qualities of your average winner;
- Qualities of your average loser;
- Winning streaks and conditions associated with it;
- Losing streaks and conditions associated with it;
- Biggest drawdown and conditions associated with it;
- Average drawdown and conditions associated with it;
- How the trades you didn't take performed;
- Reasons you didn't take those trades;
- How those reasons helped you and hurt you.

If you performed your post analysis in this way, do you think you would begin performing better or worse? The answer should be obvious. In fact, I guarantee you will improve if you continuously follow these steps.

Here's a real-life example of how I've used the above process to improve. I used to have a rule against trading thinly traded stocks. I considered any stock trading under 400,000 shares per day as thin. In fact, stocks that traded under 400,000 shares/day wouldn't even make it onto my Universe List.

As time went on and others in my circles spoke about trades they were taking, I saw a few of them taking trades I considered thin. Some would be winners. Some wouldn't. But some would blast off. *Interesting,* I thought.

Rather than adding these thinner stocks to my Universe straight away, I began tracking the ones that met every other criterion I was interested in aside from the 400,000 shares per day rule. At the time, I started to look at anything between 200k and 399,999 and tracked these trades that I didn't take.

Lo and behold, after about three months I began to notice that staying away from thinly traded stocks was hurting my performance. Sure, there were both winners and losers over the period. But this notion of "stay away from anything under 400k" was hurting me.

I began testing thinner names. As of today, I'll go down to about 75,000 shares traded per day. I take some other factors into account and will observe the general price action to see if it's something that fits my personal style, but because of this process of asking and answering questions and post analysis, I've added more winning options to my system.

Tracking all of this and being willing to do this post analysis is how we continuously question the status quo. It's how we can grow. One of the best things that can happen is when we track a trade we didn't take, write out the reasons for it, watch the trade go to the moon, and then pluck the limiting belief we had.

Planning the Road Ahead

It's from our post analysis that we discover what we need to work on next. At one point, I was the guy that would try out each new theory, routine, tool, belief set, and course. I'd get to a certain point, plateau, and then wonder if I had just spent several months, sometimes even a year or two, climbing the wrong mountain. I did some version of a post analysis, but it wasn't like the routine I just shared with you. My prior post analysis lacked intention. It lacked clarity of goals aside from "get better."

When we do a post analysis we'll find pleasure, pain, and what I call the "murky middle." The murky middle is what sends us off on all these wild goose chases. At this point, we understand that we need change. We may even want change. But to get the change we're after, the murky middle is the spot to avoid.

Go to extremes. Look at the questions we asked earlier. Our "average" serves as a baseline, but that's about it. If we want to improve, digging into our average will just get us more average. We want to dig into what is working best and what is knocking us off course the most. Pulling from those two directions will get the growth we're after, doing more of what works by understanding as much as we can about it, doing less of what doesn't by understanding as much as we can about that as well, and taking action and then repeating the process. This will assuredly reset our baseline. Our "average" then becomes better and better. Motivational speakers Tony Robbins and Ed Mylett talk about "raising standards." Gary Vaynerchuk talks about "clouds and dirt." Ancient Chinese philosophy talks about the "yin and yang." Just like how mountains are created by two land masses pushing together and raising the earth, we must pull what to do more of from our best winners, what to do less of from our worst losers, and there too shall we create our mountain of prosperity and wealth.

THREE HABITS THAT WILL HELP YOU IMPROVE

1. Accountability

So you've marked your calendar and scheduled your post-analysis sessions. But what if something happens and you feel yourself getting blown off course? Another great way to make the habit stick is by getting **accountability partners.** Accountability partners come in all shapes and sizes. This can take the form of a person whom you trust, can confide in, and will be rooting for you. This can be someone you know in person, virtually, or a mentor or coach.

There is a term psychologists use called "cognitive consonance." This is where your beliefs, words, and actions are consistent. The opposite creates cognitive dissonance, which leads to mental confusion and feeling conflicted. Humans don't like feeling conflicted.

How can we use this to our advantage? If we intentionally tell others what we plan to do, it makes us that much more likely to follow through. This is how we can leverage things such as peer groups and even social media to our advantage. Be forewarned that the flip side to sharing is that it leaves the door open for the trolls to come out to play. It may also fall on deaf ears. The main thing is that you are proclaiming your intentions to the universe. Write them down in your journal. Review your journal, and you'll continuously see those intentions. Keep them simple. One, two, or three tops until the habit is installed.

How long does it take to install a habit? About 66 days according to the experts. It's for that reason that I've created the MARA 66-Day Challenge. Grab the PDF at tradingmindwheel.com/resources.

2. Consistent "Perfect Practice"

In his book *Mindset Secrets for Winning,* my friend Mark Minervini talks about the concept of "perfect practice." This is precisely what we spoke about earlier when it comes to intent. We want to practice with the intention of improvement. Doing the same thing over and over won't get us there if we haven't practiced well. Breaking the various components of successful trading down step by step and practicing them not until you get it right, but practicing until you can't get it wrong. This is the philosophy of the famous basketball coach John Wooden.

In trading, this may look like drilling patterns with only price bars on the chart and nothing else. No indicators. No moving averages. You might even remove volume from the equation as well if you're focusing in on price action. All of those other parts add tremendous value, but if we're attempting to get better at one singular component, isolate it and work on it.

This helps us train our **RAS (reticular activating system).** In layman's terms, this is the part of the brain that helps us filter out the noise based on what's important to us. Try it for yourself right now. Think of the color blue. Repeat the word "blue" to yourself five times. Now take a look around you and see how many things you can spot that are blue.

Training ourselves to spot the patterns and finer details in trades is no different. History may not repeat itself, but it sure does rhyme. The same types of patterns will repeat themselves. How we handle them repeats itself, too. When we handle them well, we want to drill those into ourselves, and we want to anchor those feelings and emotions tied to them. Get up and celebrate. Dance around. Give yourself a high five. It may sound silly, but when we do this, it creates new anchor points in our brains and new neural pathways for those positive feelings and emotions to travel.

Likewise, we want to do similar things with the worst parts of our trading. Where the moment we see it we have a visceral reaction.

Practicing once or twice like this won't get you the trading results you're after. This is why this subsection is called "Consistent 'Perfect Practice.'" Obviously, the more of it you're able to schedule in, the better. However, start by blocking it out on your calendar just as you did earlier. You'll be 100% focused during this time. Monotasking in this way gives you the best opportunity to improve.

Through your post analysis, you'll learn what part(s) of your trading needs the most work, which skill sets must be developed. Grade yourself from 1 to 10 using the chart below (see Fig 6.1). Grab a free PDF copy of this chart by going to tradingmindwheel.com/resources.

Think of it like a wheel on a bike. A lopsided wheel won't roll so well. Work on inflating the area you're most deficient in first. Reassess, and then work on inflating the others. Keep going. If you honestly score yourself as a 10 in each category and your results match, start paying it forward if you haven't already started doing so. There are millions of people who need your help, that are trying to achieve what you have achieved. I believe the job of the most successful among us is to help serve. It's the next level, and from my experience, it's perhaps the most fulfilling part.

Here's a quick analogy to help drive home the point. Think of an apple tree. It starts out as a tiny sapling. It needs a lot of care. It takes time for it to grow. It takes even more time for it to bear fruit. Once it does start bearing fruit, it continues to grow. As it grows, it bears more and more fruit, thus serving more and more people. But it doesn't end there. Some of the seeds inside the fruit bear even more trees. A grove soon grows. All from this one fully grown apple tree that was kind enough to share its fruit. Will you be like that apple tree?

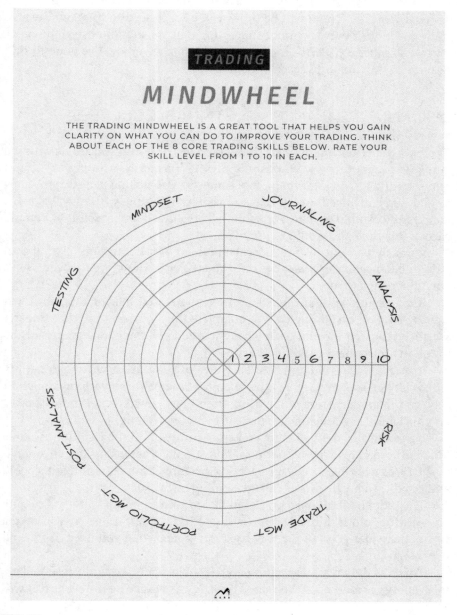

FIG 6.1

3. Discipline

Discipline is a close cousin to consistency. To me, discipline means doing the things we're supposed to be doing even when they aren't convenient. It's not always going to be convenient to block out time on the calendar and stick to doing any of this. There will be times when we'll need to miss our favorite show, activity, or event. I'm not suggesting that we should never indulge or that we completely sacrifice some of the things we enjoy. I've gone to that extreme myself, up until recently actually.

DISCIPLINE + BALANCE = SUSTAINABLE SUCCESS

There was a period where I'd sacrifice going on short mini-vacations with the family to get more work in, pushing myself constantly, wanting to achieve more, wanting to do it for them. It became so extreme that at a subconscious level, I had convinced myself that I must earn this time with my family. If I hadn't fully completed a task or achieved a result, I'd tell myself that I hadn't earned this time and would refuse to go.

We each have our own set of scales and our own definitions of what constitutes balance. If our scales are unbalanced for too long, we tip over. That's what happened to me.

It may sound silly, and I feel a little embarrassed sharing this, but I was leaning so hard on "discipline" to complete this book on time that I nearly sacrificed the first time I'd see my daughter and god-daughter experience the joy of an amusement park together.

It was a Friday, a day where I'd typically get a lot of writing done. My wife, Melissa, was putting together a day at Sesame Place with my daughter Lily, god-daughter Anna, a longtime friend and now brother-in-law Louie, and his wife, Erin. Melissa asked me if I was up to going.

Up to this point, I had barely taken any time off in the last nine months. I had refused to give myself permission to attend other events like this previously. I was working six days per week. Coaching, trading, writing this book, and building a business were all consuming me.

The thought of taking a break felt like priming a pump halfway. Imagine one of those old-fashioned water pumps from the late 1800s. If you take a break, the water goes all the way back down, and then you need to start all over again.

This was the story I was telling myself. Objectively speaking, it served me by keeping me focused. At the same time, it wasn't serving me because it was keeping me off balance and sacrificing a large part of what I was working toward: providing a better life for my family than the one I had growing up. That includes quality time with family.

When I came to this realization, I decided to give myself permission to go on this trip. I burst into tears. It had been so long since I had given myself permission to do anything like this that I was beginning to forget what it felt like. I later came to realize that this would likely be the last time we'd all be on a trip like this. Of course, we'll do lots of other things together. But when will our kids be this age again? When will they experience something magical like this for the first time together? How important is it for a child to have the presence of their parents? And how do these things compare with another 20 pages written a day earlier? Or a trade that rockets off to the moon? Or being disciplined so as to not break a streak?

These were the questions I asked myself that day. I think I made the right call.

What I learned from this experience is that part of being able to maintain discipline is by finding balance. I also learned that balance often means leaning a little more to one side than the other. It's rarely ever centered, and when it is, it doesn't last very long. If you're doing the other parts of this book already, trust your intuition and have faith.

Discipline When We Don't Want To

A great way to look at discipline is keeping the promises we make to ourselves even when it isn't convenient. If we promise ourselves we're going to wake up at a certain time, this might mean committing to hitting the snooze button one less time until we break that habit altogether. If we promise ourselves we'll go for a run but it's cold outside, discipline means we grab a jacket and head out the door.

How can we maintain this type of discipline? Balance, as we just spoke about it, is one way. Another comes in preparation. Blocking time. Coming up with contingency plans for life's curveballs. Commitment. Getting back on the horse when we're knocked off.

These words may sound all well and good. But how about some tools to help make it happen?

We're emotional creatures. Much of our actions are driven by emotion. The feeling we want to achieve. Why are you trading in the first place? A sense of financial freedom? Freedom of mobility? Achievement? Security? Abundance? Those are just a few, and there are plenty of others, but I think you get the drift. The point is that in order to follow through with discipline, we must tie high levels of emotion to what it is that we're trying to be disciplined with.

Will you be more disciplined in developing these skill sets because you read them in some book or because doing so will provide you and your loved ones the abundance and freedom you're after? On those challenging days when you're exhausted, your favorite show is on, or it's easier to head out for a few drinks, having a strong emotional commitment to discipline will keep you on track. Just remember to keep some semblance of balance as we talked about earlier.

Questions

Here are five common questions that come up during post analysis and the answers that will serve you.

1. How do I know if I'm making progress?

    The ultimate long-term metric of progress is our equity curves. If our equity curve is improving over time, we are making progress. But how often should we measure this kind of progress? What else should we measure?

There's a difference between measurement and evaluation. Think of measurement as logging the data. With this definition, most of us should measure our progress daily. Some of us may measure our progress even more frequently than that. How often we should evaluate our progress is what we're talking about in this chapter and what we discussed earlier. Ultimately you decide, but the benchmark for making that decision is "What frequency of evaluation serves you best?" For some metrics such as win rate, average gain, and average loss over the last 10 trades, I'll evaluate daily. On metrics such as the equity curve, I'll consider it monthly.

2. How do I know if I'm measuring the right things?

We know that we're measuring the right things through our experience. We gain a baseline by learning from others (such as by reading this book). Then we go out into the real world and put our knowledge to use. We experience what is serving us and what isn't. We study others. We get around others that are having better success. We get around others that are a few steps ahead of us. We learn from them and what they're measuring. We adopt it. Implement it. And repeat the process. What we start with is going to be drastically different from where we end up.

3. What if my objective changes?

Your objective will change over time. It's a matter of when, not if. Major life events such as the birth of a child or a change in career can dramatically affect our trading. Recall that in order to trade successfully, our beliefs, goals, and ability to execute must be in alignment. As much as possible, we want to plan ahead for life changes. When it comes to the birth of a child, this is fairly simple. We know we have nine months. If something happens unexpectedly such as loss of income or loss of a loved one, our trading will be affected, and you can bet that our objective will have changed. The best thing we can do in this scenario is pause and regroup and get help.

4. How often should I do a post analysis?

For optimal results, review the day at the end of the day, the week at the end of the week, the month at the end of the month. Follow the pattern for quarterly, six-month, and yearly analyses.

5. Do I need to do this alone? Can I get help?

Post analysis can be done alone. It can also be done with a partner, coach, or mentor. If working with someone else, get clear on the metrics. Understand what is being evaluated and why.

TESTING: Factor Modeling, Back Testing, and Forward Testing

To make a style, system, or strategy ours, where it's not just something we've read in a book, watched in a video, or even learned from a course, we must test it. Otherwise, they're just words and data. We need to make sure they make sense. They may have even made others hundreds of millions of dollars. But until we test it out for ourselves, it's all just words.

If trading is an art, the way to move from art enthusiast to artist is through practice.

You have all the tools necessary to become incredibly successful at trading. Now we must put them to use. We must put them to the test. We must continuously improve them. Sharpen them. And in this chapter, we'll discuss ways you can do that.

There are three types of testing that we'll discuss in this chapter. They are:

1. Factor Modeling;
2. Back Testing;
3. Forward Testing.

FACTOR MODELING

When it comes to most things in life, trading included, we do not need to reinvent the wheel. We just need to learn how to drive the car and figure out which car we like best. This is essentially what factor modeling is all about.

If you've heard the term "modeling success," you know 90% of what factor modeling is.

Factor modeling is taking a look at what already works and breaking down the reasons why. This is precisely how Nicolas Darvas discovered his "box theory" and breakout systems. It's how William O'Neil came up with CANSLIM. It's how Mark Minervini developed SEPA. It's how I crafted EAGLE.

The process is already familiar to you, and you'll have no problem doing this yourself. The process simply comes down to asking and answering questions. The better the questions we ask, the better the answers we'll be able to find.

For example, when William O'Neil was working at Hayden Stone, he asked himself the question, How are the guys over at Fidelity doing so well? He noticed that they were buying stocks as they were making 52-week highs, contrary to the popular notion of "buy low and sell high."

They were buying high and selling higher! This then led Bill to ask the question, What are the common factors among the stocks that had the biggest 1–5 year returns? That question led to what would eventually become CANSLIM and achieve some of the biggest stock market returns in history.

Like O'Neil, who struggled mightily at the beginning of his trading career, I also asked, What actually works? But instead of having to pour through mountains of raw data, I was able to find O'Neil's book *How to Make Money in Stocks*.

Success wasn't as simple as reading a book and doing what it says (as I had been trained to believe for most of my formal education). I didn't begin making real progress until about 2010, when I began asking, How can I take the work that these titans of industry have already done and make it work for me? Following along like a cookbook wasn't working for me. Trading is a mental game, and our minds are like blenders, taking in information from all over and whipping it all together. While the beliefs that others have had led to their own incredible successes, each had their own unique blend of ideas. I needed to find a way to align my mindset with one that would ultimately lead me to success.

Recall that at this point I had already dealt with "professional" mutual funds, money managers, TV celebrities, and financial gurus. I had also discovered a style that seemed to fit me well but needed a bit of custom-tailoring. We all come into the market with our own blend of beliefs. Trading is so nuanced that it's imperative for us to go through this process of assessing our beliefs because if we don't, then at best we can hope for is mediocrity. Results that are more or less in line with the market averages. If that's what we're after, then why not save ourselves all this trouble and simply buy SPY or QQQ, the ETFs that track the S&P 500 and the NASDAQ?

This question led me to a customization and refining process. The car was in my possession. I just needed to make a few adjustments to make it my own.

You may be asking yourself, If it isn't broken, why fix it?

Perhaps if we think of it more like a suit, it will help. We can buy a suit off the rack. Maybe the pants are a bit too long. Perhaps the cuffs need to be taken in a little bit. Technically the suit isn't "broken," but we do need to do a bit of tailoring to get it to fit right. So the tailor takes some measurements, logs where the suit needs to be taken in with a piece of chalk, and then gets to work.

When we find systems that we like, that fit well, we need to measure them against our beliefs, goals, and abilities to execute. From there we can begin custom-tailoring the system to ourselves.

Putting Factor Modeling to Work

Factor modeling often involves carving a new path, accepting the unknown, breaking free of our comfort zones. If we're engaging in factor modeling, we're leaving our preconceived notions at the door. We must be willing to go against what we think we know and accept the results of what we find.

Mentally, this sounds exhausting. It's no wonder then that the titans mentioned in this book including but not limited to Jesse Livermore, Nicolas Darvas, William O'Neil, and Mark Minervini all reached a certain level of frustration with the path they were previously on and had an "enough is enough" moment. They each raised their standards and committed to finding a better path. They each had powerful reasons for doing so. These reasons helped them to persevere. Writing charts by hand and looking at data on microfilm for hours on end in public libraries isn't always fun. Having a powerful why helped each of them.

What's your why?

How to Factor Model, What to Look For

A natural question that may come to you is what should we look for when factor modeling. What we should look for depends on the questions we're trying to answer. The better the questions we ask ourselves, the better and the quicker the answers we'll find.

Broad questions will give us broad answers, and that's not what we're after here.

"How can I make money investing in stocks?"

This may seem like a good question to ask. Heck, it's pretty darn close to the title of one of my favorite trading books. However, while it may be a good title for a book, it's a lousy question for us to ask ourselves. First off, it's way too broad. How many ways are there to make money investing in stocks? Literally thousands! Second, if you're honest with yourself, you probably have a few other things in mind that would make this more specific.

O'Neil wasn't just interested in making money in stocks. He was *really* interested in finding and being in stocks capable of making huge moves in a relatively short period of time of several months to a few years.

Minervini was *really* interested in asymmetric reward-to-risk opportunities while simultaneously maximizing compounding.

I was *really* interested in figuring out how I could take what I learned from these guys and adapt it to where I could execute it well while still having a day job.

We need specificity. We need focus. Here's a simple template to follow:

1. Brainstorm. Focus on your topic of interest (in this case trading), and write down anything that comes to mind that you'd like to figure out. For this part, it's okay to be broad. We'll start narrowing it down in a moment.

2. If you came up with more than five in step 1, go through your list and circle the top five ideas that intrigue you the most. If not, move on to step 3.

3. Look at your top five and narrow it down to three. If you have less than three, move to step 4.

4. From your top three, narrow it down to one.

5. From your top idea, ask it why. Try to go seven layers deep with it, and you'll not only get to the heart of what it is that you're trying to figure out, but you'll also get to the motivators behind it.

Once you have something specific that you're going to factor model, then it's time to get down to work.

To give you another example of a factor model, when I run my post analysis and ask myself, What were the common elements among my top performing trades this quarter, six months, year, and so forth? this is a form of factor modeling. I'm looking for the common factors among my best trades so I can model my future trades on what has worked best.

We've already spoken about data collection and lookback periods, so I won't go into them in great detail here. However, it is worth reiterating that being cognizant of timing, time periods, and market cycles is important whenever we're factor modeling. As is the sample size. Seeing that something occurs 10 out of 10 times may be a great start, but it's not enough to build a system around. Could you flip a coin and see it land on heads 10 times in a row? Sure! Especially if you flip the coin 1,000 times. To get robust results that we can count on, we need a large sample size. Usually, we can spot losers right away. If something isn't working after 20 times it's likely a dud, and we won't need to continue running the test to 100. But to ensure a system is solid, we need a sample of 100 minimum.

BACK TESTING

Back testing allows us to become Marty McFly from *Back to the Future*. We get to go back in time and see how our trading systems and rules would have worked out. This is a *HUGE* confidence builder. Not only that, it can save you time and a fortune.

Back testing is vital. We have the ability to see how trades or trading systems would have played out in the past. We have the great luxury of doing this without having to put any real capital to work.

Back testing can be a powerful tool, but we have to be careful with it and use it in the right way. If we don't, it can lead to a false sense of confidence, and a false sense of confidence can get us killed.

Here are the warning labels I consider when I think about back testing:

ONE: The first drawback comes from the idea that we can find factors that would produce perfect or near-perfect results. This combined with a "never settle" or "never say die" attitude is what stops most people in their tracks or sends them on wild goose hunts that last years. Sometimes lifetimes. If this feels like you, you're not alone. About 20% to 30% of the people I've worked with are similar. The good news is that there's hope and a light at the end of the tunnel. It starts with uprooting that belief about perfection. Perfection is actually the lowest possible standard we can strive toward because it doesn't exist. I challenge you to look at anyone that has had major success at anything and to see if they're perfect. On second thought, I'll save you the trouble of looking. They're not!

TWO: Curve fitting, a very close cousin to perfection. This involves attempting to create a system that would have worked great in the past and apply it to the future. What's wrong with this, you may ask? The problem is that the future is unknown, and curve fitting assumes what happened in the past will happen in the future.

A proper backtest starts with a hypothesis. It does not form a hypothesis.

So if we're not striving for perfection or even for optimization, what should we strive toward?

Progress. Progress compounds, no matter how small. Progress encounters setbacks and finds ways to overcome them. Progress wins in the long run.

As mentioned throughout this book, we want systems that match our beliefs, goals, and abilities to execute. When figuring out what to test, start there. For example, suppose you find a way that can triple your money. You find it, but it requires you to do something that you're not able or are unwilling to do.

In this case, take the Thomas Edison approach. Don't just toss it aside. Log it and archive it. It's not a failure. It's something that you may have use for later on.

Putting Back Testing to Work

Back Testing can actually build upon factor modeling. Say, for example, you've found some great rules, strategies, and tactics in this book. You'd like to see how they'd play out before putting any money into it. You can run what I call a "manual backtest."

Suppose you like the ideas laid out in the chapters on risk management and position sizing. You'd like to see how they would fit into your trading.

If you already have your trades logged in a spreadsheet, it will be very simple to go into the spreadsheet, adjust the risk parameters on your trades, and see what the results would have been. This is actually the process by which I discovered I was shooting myself in the foot by taking gains early.

I like selling into strength and still do. However, back then I was selling too much into strength. The quick gains felt good, but when I eventually had the big winner, I'd have so few shares that it would often make little impact on my bottom line. This was incredibly frustrating.

So what did I do? I raised my own standard and set out to test several different sizing strategies and several different trade management strategies. What I found was that managing my stop a bit more aggressively (getting it to breakeven sooner) and selling into strength when I get to 2× my risk yielded the best results.

Backtesting logs are fairly simple to create. If you'd like to use the ones we've developed, they're currently available as part of our coaching program. Go to tradingmindwheel.com/resources to learn more.

FORWARD TESTING

Forward testing is the process that lets us see how our trading systems and rules perform in real time. We can choose to do this with virtual money or with real money.

Suppose you wanted to test out my EAGLE strategy for yourself in real time. You would start by running the screens outlined in this book. You can find the setups and apply the sizing strategies. You can then try them out to see how they work for you. You might start out with virtual dollars. Tracking them in a charting service, broker, or spreadsheet. If it produces results that you like, then you would then move on to testing with real money.

Since you're still in the testing phase, you want to use an amount of capital that is appropriate for testing. The actual amount will vary from person to person. Whatever amount you select for yourself, it should be an amount that won't hurt you if you were to lose it all. At this point, you know enough about position sizing and risk management that "losing it all" is highly unlikely, but it's still a card in the deck no matter how unlikely it is. The amount you select should be enough that even though it won't hurt you if you lose it, you should still care about it. It should sting a little if you lose it. If you treat it in this way, you'll be as close to an actual full trading scenario as possible. In this way, it will be easier for you to transition and scale up should the test prove positive.

Putting Forward Testing to Work

Forward testing has the benefit of seeing how things play out in the here and now. It's the next logical step after back testing. To do it well, we're going to want to track our results. A great way to track these results is to use the same tracking methods that we apply to trades that we actually take. Just place a note in your log that this trade is part of the test or better yet, start a fresh log.

A way that I like to test the fine-tuning of my criteria is to track the trades that were close but didn't make the cut. I mark these a "NO TRADE" and list out the reasons why. From there I'm able to come back to them at a later time and easily see how they would have played out. Using this method played a role in how I tighten my entries and how I use intraday charts to fine-tune the trade management of my swing trades.

You can save yourself a lot of time, headache, and money by running your tests in this order. Just like everything else in this book, it goes back to mindset, beliefs, and growing a mental garden of strong beliefs.

It all starts with a seed. In this case, factor modeling is the seed. By starting with factor modeling, you're starting with something that actually works. Part of your job is deconstructing some of the why (thus the term "FACTOR" modeling). This is how you plant and begin to nurture the seed.

Once you've completed your factor models, your mental seed has begun to sprout. We want to continue nurturing that sprout. We may have a good idea here, but it's still very early in the process and not ready to bear fruit yet. Our mental sprout must be tested. The next phase, therefore, is back testing.

Back testing is the fastest, cheapest, and most robust way to run tests at this stage. You have access to endless amounts of data from which to run back tests. You don't even need any special software. You can do it for free if you really want. Some raw data from Google or Yahoo Finance and a spreadsheet are plenty to get you started. Even in this way, you'll be able to run tests fairly quickly.

If our sprout survives the back tests, it has now progressed to something that is almost ready to bear fruit. We've seen how it's worked through the different seasons and cycles of the past through back testing. Now it's time to test it out in real life. Forward testing lets us do that. We may have just one apple tree so far from this test. But if it proves successful, we can quickly scale it and soon have an entire orchard.

This is how we have a thriving mental garden. It's how we inflate the tires of our trading mindwheel. It's how we roll down the path of success.

Conclusion

At the beginning of this book we talked about how internal and external battles can sometimes cause us to become derailed. A monster we thought we had dealt with or defeated comes knocking at the door of our minds again. An external battle at work or home demands attention, shifts our focus, and temporarily halts our progress.

I want to drive home one final point.

This is life, and life will throw many curveballs at us. When this happens and you are knocked down, remember this famous quote from Rocky: "It's not about how many times you get hit. It's about how many times you get hit and keep moving forward."

We're going to get hit. Sometimes these hits may cause derailments. Following the tenets of this book will help you stay on track, but it'd be foolish to believe that we'll never get knocked off course.

We may not be able to prevent all derailments. We are going to take hits. But we choose whether or not we stay derailed. We choose if we get up. We choose if we keep moving forward.

The market is a metaphor for life. It's an infinite stream of opportunity. Seeing it that way depends on our perspective. We've been granted the freedom of choice and can choose whatever perspective we want. When we get knocked down, we can take it as the universe conspiring against us. Or we can take it as an important lesson we need to teach us how to get back up. If we get to choose our perspective, why not choose one that works? Sometimes the hardest times in our lives turn out to be our biggest blessings and exactly what we need to get to the next level.

Acknowledgments and Inspirations

Writing this book has been transformative and the journey of a lifetime for me. There are many who have contributed in ways big and small. Direct and indirect. If it weren't for them, this book probably would not exist.

First, I'd like to thank God for the opportunity to be here, to exist, and to share my story.

I'd like to thank my parents. If it weren't for them, I quite literally would not be here. As I've matured, I've come to realize that while many things were said and many actions were taken, love was always present on both sides. I'd like to thank my brother James, who I've recently reconnected with, for helping me better see this. I love you all.

I'd like to thank my stepmom, Mary, for being the mom I needed in a complicated situation that lasted for years. You're one of the strongest people I know, and I'm blessed to have you. Thank you for your love, your support, and your lasagna.

Thank you to my sister Dana. You've had such an impact on me through the years. You're a blessing, and I love you.

To my uncle Francis, thank you for our many talks. Most especially that talk on the way home from Gino's all those years ago. It's what sparked my interest in the stock market.

I'm quite grateful for my entire family, extended family, and in-laws. I would not be who I am today without you. Thank you, and please know that I love you all.

Thank you to John Jenks, my office mate, who encouraged me to give trading one more shot and introduced me to the works of William O'Neil and Investor's Business Daily.

Thank you to Adam Sarhan for your support through the years, for being a colleague, and for being a friend. You were one of the first to encourage me to transform my passion for trading into something more. How far we've both come since then!

Thank you to Beth Marconi. Your support and guidance were critical when I was on the edge and needed it most. Who knows how this story might have ended if it weren't for your help at that most delicate juncture. Thank you.

Thank you to the long and ever-growing list of teachers, coaches, mentors, and aspirational mentors. Most especially Mark Minervini, William O'Neil, Van Tharp, Mark Douglas, Jim Roppel, Stan Weinstein, Mike Webster, Charles Harris, Avi Fogel, Curt Hostetter, Richard McKay, Jim Duggan, Ajay Jani, Patrick Walker, Evan Carmichael, Jason Fonceca, Tyron Grandison, Douglas Lackey, Gerrit Kamperdyke, Joseph Russo, Mark Van Schenkhof, Tony Robbins, Brendon Burchard, Robin Sharma, Jim Kwik, and Ed Mylett.

Thank you to all of our clients, students, and followers through the years. Your support means the world to me. If I've been able to help you a fraction of the amount you have helped me, I know we're making a huge difference.

Thank you to Susan Cerra, Kevin Harreld, and the entire team at Wiley. Thank you for the opportunity to work with you on this book, your incredible levels of support and encouragement, the numerous extensions, and for keeping us on track.

Thank you to Stuart Chalmers. You've been a great friend, colleague, and confidant. You inspire me, and I am better for knowing you.

Thank you to Gerik Goncalves. Our friendship means the world to me. We grew up together. We've built businesses together. What we've built through the years has been awe-inspiring. You are truly my right hand.

To my daughter Lily, I love you more than words can express. I find myself loving you more and more each day. Thank you for all the joy you bring. You truly inspire me. Thank you for being you.

And finally, to my beloved beautiful wife, Melissa. You believed in me, this work, and us from the start. You believed through the many challenges we've faced. You've encouraged, edited, guided, coached, and cheerled. You supported, loved, and lifted me even when times were tough. You're an endless source of inspiration; I couldn't have done any of this without you. Thank you. I love you.

One final word.

Big or small, we never know the impact we will have. Our job is to show up each day and always give our best. God bless.

About the Author

Michael Lamothe is a highly successful trading coach who has blended his unique experiences with a diverse set of practical strategies that have made him a sought-after speaker and leader within the financial industry today.

Michael earned both his BBA and MBA from Baruch College in New York City. As a young academic, he won awards in philosophy, which would later serve as a springboard for deeper research into mindset, beliefs, psychology, and history.

Michael had tried and failed at trading financial markets for years. He had nearly given up, but at a colleague's urging, he gave it one last shot. He read the works of William O'Neil and became a part of the local Investor's Business Daily Meetup chapter in NYC. Within a year he was profitable and invited to be a leader in that group. He held that leadership position for a decade.

After becoming profitable in the market, trading part time while still maintaining a separate full-time career, Michael launched his first business to help others find success while trading part time. This led to speaking gigs across the United States including events hosted by StockTwits in Coronado, California, American Association of Individual Investors (AAII) in St. Louis, Missouri, and multiple appearances on NASDAQ TV.

As success continued to build for Michael both in trading and as an early-stage entrepreneur, he co-developed software and stock screening tools and developed a series of online courses and training. He was a finalist in Benzinga's Global Fintech Competition.

Before the age of 40, Michael left the corporate world behind to pursue entrepreneurship and to coach others full time in trading with a focus on mindset and skill development.

Michael's passion led him to write a best-selling book and amass a social media following of more than 150,000 across Instagram, Twitter, and StockTwits (@MichaelGLamothe). He has partnered with investing clubs to educate and help people trade better. Michael enjoys engaging with his followers and is active on several social media platforms where his posts are regularly viewed hundreds of thousands of times each month.

As a coach, Michael has helped thousands of people. He is known for combining mindset, beliefs, and philosophy alongside tactics and strategies that are able to help people get real results in their trading.

Michael is very humble about his successes and believes that God and the universe always have his back. Tough times, struggles, and challenges are all meant to serve if we allow them to. Once Michael adopted this philosophy, his life started to move toward the next level.

In his free time, Michael is a health and fitness enthusiast. He enjoys the arts, fine wine, and music. He and his wife Melissa are proud parents to their daughter Lily.

Index

Page numbers followed by *f* refer to figures.